SUFFERING

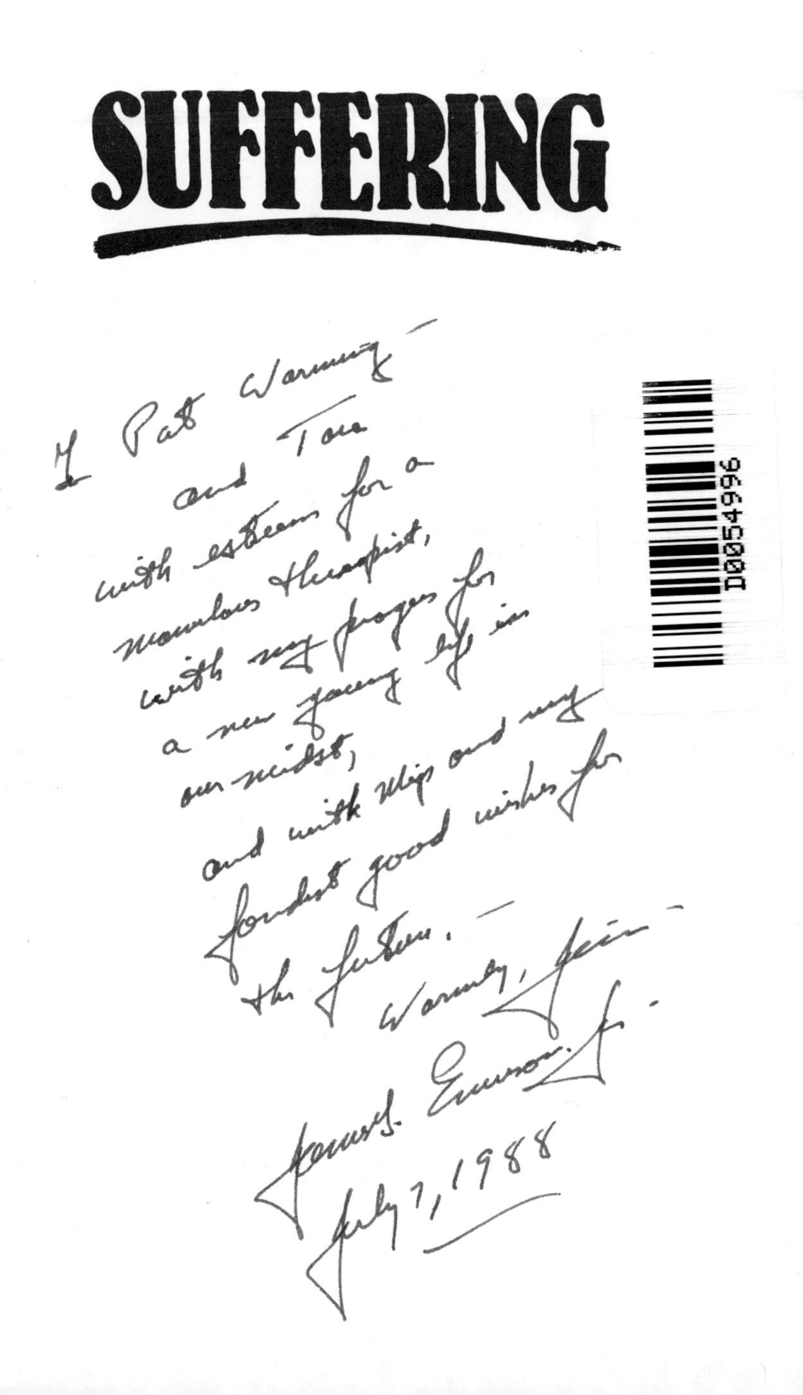

SUFFERING

ITS MEANING AND MINISTRY

James G. Emerson

Abingdon Press
Nashville

Suffering: Its Meaning and Ministry

This book is printed on acid-free paper

Library of Congress Cataloging-in-Publication Data

EMERSON, JAMES G. (James Gordon), 1926–
Suffering: its meaning and ministry.
Includes index.
1. Suffering—Religious aspects—Christianity.
2. Suffering. I. Title
BT732.7.E47 1986 231′.8 85-28978

ISBN 0-687-40573-4 *(pbk.: alk. paper)*

MANUFACTURED BY THE PARTHENON PRESS AT
NASHVILLE, TENNESSEE, UNITED STATES OF AMERICA

To the members of my family, who have known suffering and who see ministry to suffering in their chosen fields of endeavor—

my wife, *Margaret Bonnell Emerson*

our sons and daughter,
John Bonnell
Lynne Edith
James Edward

and our son-in-law,
David Arnold Phillips

I dedicate this book

CONTENTS

PREFACE

Suffering requires care. But suffering itself may bring a form of care. The discovery of this strange contradiction led to the writing of this book.

In reviewing my notes for this book, I feel gratitude—indeed indebtedness—to many people: those who were willing to be interviewed, those who have written and shared their suffering, and those people of the past and present who have had an impact on my life and have helped me come to terms with suffering.

This book was begun because of the Reverend Glenda Hope of the Network Ministries in San Francisco. Her invitation to teach a course on urban suffering in the alternative seminary program of the Pacific School of Religion led me once again to pull my thoughts and practice together. This unique program of the school combines "hands on" experience with seminar reflection in ways that allow for a needed integration of faith and work. The students and I both learned in this experience.

The encouragement to continue this process came from Chaplain William O. Smith of Fort Sanders hospital in Knoxville, Tennessee. Thanks to his affirmation, and that of the Reverend W. Edmund

Carver, D.D., I was invited to develop those ideas for presentation at the Gammon Lectures of that hospital.

From the experience of both groups, I have written this book—not just for clergy, but for all who seek to help people in their moments of suffering. Especially, however, I have in mind those people who combine faith in God with the need to help in what I call *the suffering moment*. I assume the reader has some interest in helping others who suffer and desires to take seriously both biblical and psychological insights in preparing himself or herself as a care giver.

In the preparation of this book, I am especially indebted to five people who read the entire manuscript: Dr. Sandra Brown of Princeton Theological Seminary, whose own background in pastoral care proved particularly helpful to me in thinking through the import of this work for the field of pastoral care; Dr. Scott Hope of San Francisco State University, whose editorial guidance and critique were superb; Mrs. Audrey Lightbody, whose response gave me the needed perspective of a person aware of my field but not professionally in it; and my wife, Dr. Margaret Bonnell Emerson, whose clinical expertise as a therapist and understanding of the "shadow" concept helped me with the fundamental insight this book brings about the suffering healer.

Finally, I remember with appreciation and affection the late Dr. Seward Hiltner, without whose encouragement and confidence my career and study in the field of care never would have begun or come to fruition; Dr. John Sutherland Bonnell, who as a teacher and later as my father-in-law, first introduced me to the field of counseling; Dr. James I. McCord, who gave me the opportunity to develop and grow as a teacher and writer by inviting me to numerous adjunct appointments at Princeton Theological Seminary;

the late Dr. James Rank, whose Christian counseling carried me through my own dark night of the soul; and Dr. Peter Rutter, whose expertise in extended consultation gave me profound insight into the approach of C. G. Jung and the role of symbols in our lives.

Any writing must be the responsibility of the author; I take that responsibility. May the reader have a measure of the benefit from reading these pages that I have gained from writing them.

James G. Emerson

San Francisco

1986

INTRODUCTION

A Ministry to the Suffering

To suffer for the sake of suffering is sick; to avoid suffering for the sake of comfort leads us to lose touch with reality. To suffer for the sake of integrity brings us to health and gives evidence of health.

I write for the person who would help in the moment of suffering: parent or child, professional or lay. I also write for the person in the midst of suffering, and that could be any one of us. All who care for those who suffer also suffer. "Suffering work" is felt by both those who suffer and those who would help. Both the sufferer and the helper must grasp what is involved, what works; for there is a difference between suffering that leads to health and suffering that destroys.

Five writings serve as background for this small book: the Bible, with emphasis on the Psalms, Job, and the experience of Christ; *J. B.* by Archibald MacLeish; *Death Camp to Existentialism* by Viktor Frankl; *Night* by Elie Wiesel; and *Suffering* by Dorothee Sölle.[1] I mention these contemporary writers for a specific reason: All wrote with an awareness of the Holocaust of the Jews.

There has been and continues to be suffering equal to theirs; but that time of hell for a people marks the western world as no other horror. No westerner, in seeking to understand suffering and ministry to suffering, can be the same person with the Holocaust in his or her background. Whether from a sense of guilt, horror, anger, or compassion, awareness of the Holocaust makes us different. (Those of a historical bent will understand also that the writings of Søren Kierkegaard have guided me personally in moments of my own hurt and struggle.)

Out of the individualism of the American frontier, there grew a view that only individuals suffer. Suffering almost contradicted the American dream. In the 1960s, the so-called Me Generation always asked, "Why does this happen to me?" Suffering shattered the dream. Today, as one seeks to deal with the reality of a holocaust—be it in the memorial buildings of a Dachau or the village of the poorest of the poor in India—the pronoun must change. No longer can we ignore the reality: Groups suffer, not just individuals. Corporate suffering is real. The one who would help hears the cry, "Why *us*, O Lord, why *us*?"

Suffering is therefore both individual and corporate. The Holocaust made that clear, and so does the massive situation in India today. As my wife and I sat in the Punjab and listened to stories of the migration that followed the formation of Pakistan, as we walked through villages of the poorest of the poor, as we talked with those in the slums, that fact was inescapable. Those of us who would minister to people in suffering must minister to corporate as well as to individual suffering.

Since the person called to heal may be reaching out to either the individual or the group, the following chapters look at an enlarged view of suffering—the suffering of a person and the suffering of a people. The people may be a family that has lost a home, a group of unemployed workers whose company has been closed, a village people who are destitute, a nation that is ravaged by earthquakes of natural or human origin. The issue is the same in each case: "How does the healer heal not only individual but also corporate bodies?"

In response to that question (I say "response," for one can never give a full answer), the first chapter looks at suffering defined—its nature and meaning. The second chapter expands the discussion by considering biblical views of suffering. Chapter 3 then turns to our emotional needs—especially as suggested by helpful observers such as Dr. Abraham Maslow—and examines them to discover the help actually required in a moment of suffering.

Although we will have looked at some examples in the prior chapters, in Chapter 4 we will consider specific cases of personal and corporate suffering—examples from India in a place of poverty and from the United States in the agony of an assassination; examples of an individual with untouchable spinal pain and another dying of a new and incurable disease. We will look to see what helped and what did not, and to understand something of suffering as we encounter it. In that context we can then touch on the ever-gnawing question, "Why do people suffer?" We will ask, "What is the meaning, for us who would help, of the suffering we have seen?"

Then and only then will I raise the question of the healer. Who are you as a healer, and who am I? Each of us heals; each of us needs healing. Some might think we should begin with this issue. Yet I feel that, since the healer also has suffered and will suffer, we cannot ask that question until we have looked at dimensions of suffering itself.

A solid foundation of biblical understanding forms both the undergirding of this book and a basis for strategy in dealing with suffering. The Bible itself contains case studies of corporate and personal suffering that have much to contribute to our understanding. Unfortunately, too many people read the Bible either just as dogma or just as literature. The Bible must also be read for its dynamic understanding of the human experience and the experience of belief. Therefore, the second chapter of this book looks at Scripture, and the sixth chapter lifts it up again as a means of integrating the whole in addressing the issue of strategy. An Epilogue dealing with implications for the future in both research and theological thought concludes the book.

Before we move to the definition of suffering in Chapter 1, two preliminary yet critical observations, which relate also to the Epilogue, must be made:

1. Liberation theology, practical theology, and humanistic psychology all address the issue of suffering. When we begin with suffering itself, however, I believe the outcome shows the need, not for any one of those schools of thought, but for a theology of responsibility. Such a theology asks, "How do we deal responsibly with suffering?" and "How do we act responsibly, once freed from suffering?" These questions raise the moral dimension in the helping professions—questions profoundly addressed by Dr. Donald Browning of the University of Chicago.[2]

2. *Suffering work* is the key technical term we must understand if we are to learn both how to help those who suffer and the role suffering plays in life.

Consider the phrase *suffering work*. Suffering work is the work done to move through a situation of pain to a moment of healing. The idea for the phrase comes from Freud's understanding of dreams and "dream work." In dream work, a dream allows sleep in spite of a whole host of pleasant and unpleasant material. A dream takes that material and puts it into symbolic form that we can handle.

In the same way, suffering work transforms a painful, hurtful, destructive situation into a process for health, well being, wholeness. We will see an example of this suffering work in each chapter. Suffering work is not evil. Rather, it is what we do to cope with evil. That insight is basic to understanding why we suffer, to answering "Why do bad things happen to good people?" or "Why must I go through this?"

The examples in these chapters are taken from literature, from work with students in my classes, from my work in pastoral counseling, and from my personal experience.

In the instance of suffering, some of what I have learned has grown not only out of seeking to help, but also out of some deeply troubled moments when I suffered, was helped, and was healed. The helpful response to suffering can come as much from the sufferer as from the healer!

What follows also makes assumptions. Space hardly allows for enumeration of these assumptions, much less comment, without writing another book! A key assumption holds that we are not merely isolated individuals. We are all in relation—in relation to nature, or other people, or memories, or institutions, or hopes, or God. Technical theories which deal with this reality are called systems theory or field theory or gestalt theory. Perhaps this assumption finds its best expression in John Donne's poem:

> No man is an Island, intire of It selfe; every man is a peece of the Continent, a part of the maine. If a

> clod bee washed away by the Sea, Europe is the lesse, as well as if a Promitorie were; . . . any man's death diminishes me, because I am part of Mankinde; And therefore never send to know for whom the bell tolls; It tolls for thee. (*Devotions*, XVII)

With that definition of suffering work and this assumption that we are all part of one another, let us turn to the question, "What is suffering?"

CHAPTER I

Suffering: Its Nature, Meaning, and Necessity

People respond to the suffering of others in several ways. Whether discussing individuals who suffer or great groups of people—as in the Holocaust—the emphasis here centers on what either individuals or groups may do to help in the suffering moment. Further, we will ask what the suffering moment itself teaches, means, or contributes to the healing process.

One approach not discussed here is revolution. The Christian foundation for the revolutionary approach has come about largely since the Reformation. John Knox in Scotland laid a theological base for corporate action against the crown. John Witherspoon built upon that base, as did countless sermons of the early 1700s in the colonies of America, and it became the undergirding for revolution as a Christian act.

Today liberation theology, more than practical theology, deals with the possibility of revolt as a means of ministry. As a later chapter states, we require structures in society that will allow us to handle suffering. On the grand scale of society, liberation theology deals with suffering by looking at changes in structure—be those structures economic, political, militaristic, or ecclesiastical. Liberation theology therefore considers the possibility of social or political revolution. I too assume the necessity of structural change, but here we will not go into the issue of revolt as a means of change.

Liberation theology has contributed much and brought much to the surface that needs discussion. Nevertheless, I have two concerns: (1) In the sweep of the theological enterprise, liberation theology has not seen its full place as being a practical theology rather than a systematic theology; (2) liberation theology deals with the sociological dimensions of the problem, but has given little attention to the psychological.

As practical theology has spoken to the liberation of the soul, liberation theology has spoken to the liberation of community, society, and culture. As a theology that emerges out of South America, liberation theology parallels the practical theology that has emerged out of North America. Liberation theologies are influenced by philosophies of sociology and economics—including the work of Karl Marx, Friedrich Engels, and others. Practical theology is influenced by philosophers of psychology and education—Freud, Jung, Rogers.

The similarity between these theologies grows from their practical base—or I would prefer to say "pastoral base." Neither are theologies in the sense of systematic, or what Seward Hiltner called logic-centered disciplines.[1] Both are the standpoints from which the systematic doctrines of God, the Church, Christ, the Trinity, and mission are understood. Both must speak to the logic-centered disciplines and hear those disciplines. Neither must make the mistake of assuming that it is a substitute for the logic-centered disciplines.

Both liberation and practical theology deal with suffering. Their concern for suffering gives them a common base and requires a mutual recognition.

Liberation theology and practical theology must be aware of each other as they deal with the issue of suffering.

With that acknowledged, however, in these chapters I focus not on liberation theology's side of the suffering experience, but on the side of practical theology. When these chapters are finished, however, we must consider the implications of this focus for the relation between what I consider to be two pastoral theologies.

I

From that background, we now look at suffering itself.

Suffering does not happen to us; we choose to suffer. Strange, even outrageous as that statement seems, it is the key to understanding suffering and ministering to those who suffer.

We must be clear about the difference between suffering and pain. Part of the difficulty in ministering is a result of confusing the two experiences. Pain happens to us. Pain is the result of being hit, hearing an unkind comment, being disappointed. Pain is the consequence of a loss, a death, a tragedy. We may sometimes choose pain—as when we agree to surgery. Usually we do not choose it—as when we are in a car accident.

Suffering, by contrast, is what we choose to do with pain. *Suffering,* according to the dictionary, is a synonym for *enduring*. To endure pain, to put up with an alcoholic husband or wife, to go to jail for what is right—these are aspects of suffering. These we choose to do. Complex as the process of making a choice becomes, choice becomes our option.

Some ask, "Does a child caught by a napalm bomb choose it? Does an infant torn from a mother's arms and impaled on a soldier's sword choose it? Does a person born in the depths of poverty make that choice?"

Those of us who have sat with a child in the heart of the slums can identify with those questions. Yet in the slums we have also seen the miracle of human resilience. That miracle reveals itself in the capacity even of children to suffer—to *choose* to suffer rather than give up. The more I read studies of early childhood, the more I wonder if we do not underestimate the degree of choice that can be found at early levels of life.

Yet the problem does not center on the degree of choice. The problem centers on the reality of evil in the world. Evil destroys. Evil destroys integrity, personality, the soul. Evil destroys relations. When Jesus asked the demoniac his name, the demoniac said, "I am Legion" (Mark 5:9). The integrity and oneness of his soul had been fractured, scattered. Choice then emerged. The demoniac maintained the dialogue with Jesus. The demoniac did not commit suicide. Jesus had a choice. Jesus chose to put the evil elsewhere. The story troubles some moderns, but none should ignore the message—the problem lay in evil, and the issue is what we choose to do with evil.

Any look at suffering must acknowledge the reality of evil and the necessity of deciding what to do with the evil once acknowledged. At whatever level of consciousness we have, we still must respond to that evil with a certain degree of awareness. We may choose to die rather than suffer (endure). We may choose to betray or blame another rather than assume a burden ourselves. In the book of Genesis, Adam chose to blame Eve and Eve chose to blame the serpent, rather than assume responsibility for their actions (Gen. 3). We choose whether or not to suffer.

Suffering means that we are free. The biblical story of creation carries the message that we are created in God's image. If God creates, then those created in God's image also have the capacity to be creative—are free to be creative. To suffer means we are in God's image, are creative human beings, not just determined bits of protoplasm. Freedom to suffer guarantees our freedom. Such freedom marks the reality of human life. None of us likes to suffer; but if we could not suffer, that would be the horror. We then would lose the capacity to suffer. Lose that capacity and we truly lose. I think of two examples:

I think of a dying woman. She was comatose. She could not respond. A comatose person seems unconscious, yet hears. The doctor said, "Your son is on his way from Japan." It took him a week to arrive. Despite the pain that drugs could not touch, the woman lived until the son returned. Within an hour after he had knelt by her bed, she died; but her choice of suffering gave her the victory of a last visit.

Another mother had Hodgkins disease. In the midst of that, her family was evicted from its apartment. The family members would not tell anyone their problems and never discussed the issues openly among themselves. They told everyone there were no problems. There was massive denial of the pain, until . . . one of the family members stepped in front of a train. Suicide meant refusal, unwillingness, or inability to suffer. The loss of capacity to suffer went hand in hand with loss of life. "Lose the capacity to suffer and we truly lose."

For the survivors, the suicide broke through the facade of composure and forced them to look at the problems. Whereas they had avoided suffering, now they chose to suffer. For the young woman, however, the issue was over. The act of suicide meant an end to suffering, but also an end to life.

Although these two events are subject to various interpretations, no one could tell the son in the first story that his mother did not choose to suffer until he arrived. The choice might have been her gift of love to him. After he arrived, with her love expressed, she could let go of life. A time would have come when she could not have held on; but the fact is, she did.

By contrast, in the second example, the family members clearly chose not to face the pain. They chose not to suffer. As a result, they did not discuss the problems of the illness or the eviction from the house. Tears and anger and fear were not allowed. Something had to break. It did. The daughter could not handle the pent-up emotions. Her suicide may have expressed anger by saying, "You'll be sorry now that I'm dead." The suicide may have said, "Now you will have to pay attention to my hurt." We do not know its message. We do know that the choice to avoid suffering pushed the family until one died and the rest finally accepted suffering.

From these two examples, note that the issue of suffering shifts from the question of why we suffer. The real issue in suffering is not "Why do bad things happen to good people?" but "How do we respond to pain and problems?" In the following chapters, that theme will occur again and again.

For further elaboration of the point, consider the case of Edith, which demonstrates one person's choice to suffer, and her victory because of that choice.

II

Edith was fifty-two years old. She was bright—a theologian, and one of my colleagues in teaching.

Although she died of cancer, for those of us who experienced her last days, she was more than a cancer statistic. In many ways, Edith had never found that niche in life that would make the best use of her considerable talents. She had been active in NOW, in civil rights with Martin Luther King, and in a host of other activities. She had had good teaching positions but had left them for various reasons. Some students and friends proved fiercely loyal to her. Others could not handle her "liberal" views. At the time of this story, she was teaching in a community college. She could have been on a graduate faculty or the educational staff of a large church. It was at the college level, however, that she found her audience.

When Edith learned she had cancer, she sent for me. Even though Edith had left my parish and joined the congregation of the Episcopal Cathedral some years before, the call did not surprise me. Our ages were the same, we knew the same professors, we admired the same theological giants. We had our differences of view, but those differences led only to a mutual respect for each other. When the call came, I went.

(My visit had her priest's blessing. The relationship shared by her priest, Edith, and others of the theological community made it most natural that any of us would have responded to such a request from any of the others.)

Upon entering the hospital room, I found Edith sitting upright in a chair and looking as though she were eight months pregnant. A student was with her. In fact, a group of students had prepared a rotation so that someone could be with Edith most of each day. The students had become family—an extended family.

Edith asked the student to leave us alone and we talked. She spoke of her pain. Edith's cancer was inoperable. The pain was tremendous. Death appeared inevitable. She felt that with meditation and relaxation exercises, she could control the pain. She wanted to be conscious. She did not want to lose the ability to communicate because of using drugs. Part of our conversation follows:

Edith 1: I am going to die, Jim.

Jim 1: I know.

Edith 2: You are one of the few out here who understands where I come from—you know Union, Tillich . . . you understand me. (silence) I need to talk with you. Can we talk?

Jim 2: Yes, I am here.

Edith 3: I am not afraid to die, but I feel sad. There is much I would like to do.

Jim 3: It is the break with all you know, isn't it; and coming at the wrong time.

Edith 4: Yes, but I want this to be a statement.

Jim 4: You mean your sickness now?

Edith 5: Well, partly, but more, the death and the funeral. That is why I want the the funeral in the Episcopal Church. The liturgy says something for me.

(Edith was a specialist in the Church of the Middle Ages. She had a profound sense of symbols. The liturgy expressed her theology as much as didpreaching.)

Jim 5: Yes, it does. I know what you mean.

Edith 6: So I want the Dean to conduct the service; but I want you to make the statement for me. I want them to remember what is important.

Jim 6: It is important to put this all together the right way so that it is an integrity with you.

Edith 7: Yes; that is why you must do it. I need for you to get Tillich's *Courage to Be*—especially the last chapter.

Jim 7: The "God Beyond God."

Edith 8: Yes, but more than that. There are some thoughts in those last few pages that really hit. Please bring them and read them and let us talk about them.

Jim 8: I will . . . then we can pull it together as you deal with this now and as I represent you then.

Edith 9: (silence; tears) I am grateful. This is going to be all right. Thank you.

Jim 9: Would you like us to pray before I go?

Edith 10: Yes.

Jim 10: With eyes closed, let us be aware of the pain, but not hold on to it; let us be aware of the sounds but not hang on to them; let us be aware of God's presence in whatever way that presence is real to us. Now, Lord, support us both in these moments. As Edith moves into this new and strange experience, allow her to sense that she is not alone, but that a Providence moves with her now, even as in years that are past. Help me as I accept the trust given in these moments that I, with her, may be faithful to your presence and that we may both discover in a new way the courage to be. We ask this in Christ's name, for he has been where we are. Amen.

I saw Edith several times. We shared emotions and thoughts. In the three weeks before she died, she took medication only twice. Anger came, and she worked through that anger. Peace came, and she died quietly in her chair. A student sat nearby, looked up, went over to kneel by the chair, and then closed Edith's eyes.

III

What happened in this experience with Edith . . . with me?

Edith needed "to be." Her personal integrity stood out clearly. "To be," in her integrity, was critical. Drugs could have robbed her of that opportunity. An overly dominant friend or chaplain could have robbed her. A hospital or doctor that did not recognize her rights as a patient could have denied her the privilege of her identity and her integrity.

In this process, Edith had a choice. She chose to endure the pain and be aware. That choice allowed her to maintain her sense of being. She did not use medication, meditation, or relaxation to escape the pain, but to control it. Yet she had alternatives. Edith could have chosen a quick way out: the short end of a rope, the gas jet at home, the overdose of pills. Instead, she chose to suffer in order to maintain who she really was. That did not mean she never took a pill. Rather, her goal was "being." There was a time when the pain became so intense that it stood in the way of her goal. Hurts can be so great that we are not ourselves. For Edith, the guideline on drugs was not the absence of pain, but the freedom to be. Suffering, for her, was that opportunity "to be." Suffering meant not the absence of cancer, but the discovery of what I like to call *wholeness of soul*.

Wholeness of soul comes from the biblical understanding of perfection. When Jesus said, "Be ye therefore perfect" (Matt. 5:48), and again when he said, "It is finished" (John 19:30), he used the word for wholeness, completeness. The goal of the gospel lies not in miracles or magic but in this wholeness—this perfection. Sometimes this wholeness will be reflected in healing. Sometimes a healing will lead to the wholeness. We do not understand the full mystery of this relationship. Nevertheless, the two must not be confused. The goal refers to salvation, which does not mean saving the body but saving the soul. The promise of the Christian message lies in wholeness of soul, despite what may happen to the body.

Edith, then, was losing wholeness of body, but she claimed her wholeness of soul. That wholeness had many dimensions. Part of wholeness of soul and part of "being" have a cosmic dimension. The cosmic dimension is always there, but not always recognized.

What is the cosmic dimension? This cosmic dimension is our awareness that we are part of something that is greater than we are. Some people have no sense of anything greater than themselves. Others have a sense of being part of a group, a country, even the world. Patriotism is a way of recognizing that one is part of something greater than oneself—for which one might die. Sadly, for some people, the nation is the greatest dimension they recognize; for other people, it is their company; and for still others, the school or local church. For Edith, this cosmic dimension was a sense of all creation, which has as its essence, God.

Any cosmic dimension carries with it a set of values, fundamentals of life, the basis on which all decisions are made, whether one is consciously aware of them or not. Karen Horney called this a "pride system." Martin Luther once wrote that whatever we set our hearts to, names our god.

Everyone has a cosmic dimension. The problem comes when that dimension is too small to deal with the pain a person is facing. When people cry out, "Why does God let this happen to me?" they may disclose that their cosmic dimension is not big enough to allow for handling the problem—to allow for healthy suffering or suffering work. Guilt, fear, idolatry, lack of courage to face reality, defensiveness—all may stand in the way of a full cosmic view. As we shall see in subsequent chapters, we must protect against the narrow view if we hope to cope with pain and allow for the best in "suffering work."

Edith's cosmic view proved adequate. It needed reaffirmation. Her interest in Paul Tillich's book provided that affirmation. An intellectual, Edith was not asking for stimulation of the mind or a technical theological discussion. Her interest in Tillich's writings helped her come to terms with the cosmos, the universe in which she had a sense of belonging.

At one point, Tillich speaks of coming to the edge of an abyss in life when we simply must have courage. Edith stood on that edge as death approached. She sought to bring that awareness into her thinking. What she once read and discussed intellectually she now experienced emotionally. For the sake of her soul, her integrity, she wanted to hear those words of the God who stands beyond our view of God. She wanted to sense the new meaning and the new understanding there for her.

From a suffering standpoint, a healthy cosmic dimension brings awareness that there are things we cannot control. We cannot know all the answers. We cannot have all the evidence for making a decision in life. Whether in facing death or making a difficult decision, there are moments when we look out into an abyss, a void. To look into that abyss and to act, we must have courage—what Paul Tillich called "the courage to be."[2]

For Edith, the sense of God gave her a sense that in the abyss, there was One who was on her side. Aware of that One, she could choose to suffer. More than that, she chose to suffer the pain because, for her, to lose the sense of the pain meant also losing that sense of God. (This observation does not mean that we must never avoid pain. It does mean that we must guard against those ways of avoiding awareness of pain which cause us to lose awareness of everything else—including God.)

At this point in Edith's experience, healing relations with others emerged as important. The prospect of losing those relations brought its own pain. "Good-bye" does not come easily. With some people she knew, there may have been tension and anger to overcome. With others, there may have been words left unsaid. With still others, "letting go" may have been the hardest part. All these areas of feeling need acknowledgment.

Rather than deal with these important matters, there is often a tendency to isolate those who are suffering, or to isolate oneself when suffering. Personally, when I am sick, I have often said, "Leave me alone on my own bed." Edith had the lure of isolation, too, but she resisted it. She chose suffering.

Sensitivity to the feeling of wanting to be alone has its place. However, we must also look realistically at the place of human or support-group relations in times of suffering. The presence of the students gave Edith a touch of the world. She could speak of her feelings—of both failure and success. With the students, with her family, with the clergy, she was able to talk through her guilts and discover a genuine sense of forgiveness.

The students helped this process, as did I, by seeking to lift up what Edith felt as well as what she said. The analysis of an interview, I will hold for a later chapter. Here, however, note that the attempt was made in each response, and in the prayer, both to lift up her feelings or thoughts and to respond to them. As the pastor, I sought not to see this as a moment to stand passively aside and allow the patient to work through her feelings. We did not have endless time. Rather, I sought to become involved in the moment with Edith, share the feelings, and respond to what was shared. In this way, I attempted to let Edith know where I stood and to communicate that I knew where she stood.

The chapter on the healed healer looks at what happens to the care giver in such a moment. Now, simply note that the friend, minister, helper, must also suffer. I was experiencing my own sense of grief and loss—anticipatory grief, it is called. Further, as one who knew Tillich's work, I found myself identifying with Edith's sense of being at the brink of an abyss. I could have been more responsive to my own awareness, but I did not because I sought to remain focused on Edith and her awareness.

Edith also had to handle her relations with herself. Her body was failing her—that body on which she had counted all these years no longer could sustain her. She looked and felt bloated. She needed those quiet times or times with another when she could express and accept her feelings about herself both physically and spiritually. She needed that which allowed for wholeness during her suffering (Heb. 2:10).

IV

Why did this happen to Edith? What was her real battle here?

Many speak easily of such illness as a sign of punishment. Others feel that it shows lack of faith. Both views are dangerous; they assume that we know much more about the mystery of faith and God's love than we do. Neither do those two views fit for those of us who knew Edith's profound faith—they do not fit the biblical sense of the forgiveness that grows in the God of love.[3]

Greek drama provides us with a helpful insight—the tragic flaw. The tragic flaw is something which represents both strength and weakness within a character or a group in a Greek drama. For instance, Oedipus in *Oedipus Rex* has a flaw—a flaw which represents both strength and weakness, and which leads to destruction.

At the risk of sounding sacrilegious, God also has a tragic flaw! God's strength is that God, who created all, has allowed for freedom. Freedom is necessary for both responsibility and individuality. The strength of freedom lies in the capacity to create. The tragic flaw in freedom centers in its use to destroy. Freedom means just that—freedom. Thus the freedom to create means also the freedom to destroy.

Because of the radical nature of the freedom we are given, the Old Testament periodically suggests that God created evil. God did not really create evil as such. Yet, by creating freedom, God created the possibility for evil. Those psalms (22, 76, and others) that ask why God withholds divine fury, those prophets (Isa. 45:7) who suggest that God created evil, identify the tragic flaw in the freedom God gives to all.

Yet neither the Old Testament nor the New holds God responsible for the evil things God's creation does with freedom; rather, the Bible makes clear that there is such a thing as evil in the world. Take away the tragic flaw in freedom, the *possibility* for evil, and one takes away the reality of both freedom and responsibility.

The fact of cancer in Edith is the fact of cells that were free to be healthy, but which for some reason had run wild, overused their ability to create, and thus caused great harm. The cancer cell may be the result of either natural evil or human evil. Whatever the explanation, the result is demonic. For Edith, then, dealing with cancer became a secondary issue. For her, maintaining her identity as a person in the face of that which was destroying her body rose as the primary issue. That battle expressed itself in the fight against concerns other than those of flesh and blood. Depression, anger, bitterness, destruction of the identity—these stand far above what happens to the flesh. As Paul said, "We wrestle not against flesh and blood, but against principalities, against powers" (Eph. 6:12). Luther picked up the same theme in his hymn "A Mighty Fortress Is Our God": "The body they may kill; God's truth abideth still." Death was not the issue for Edith. The issue was that she not be destroyed by the destroyer.

The opera *Faust* by Gounod provides a parable of Edith's problem. In that opera, Faust trades his soul to Mephistopheles for freedom from old age. At the end of the opera, Faust asks Marguerite to go with him into the realms of hell. Marguerite refuses the easy way out. Mephistopheles shouts to Faust, "Condemned." As Faust collapses, Marguerite moves serenely into the realm of heaven, and Mephistopheles also collapses. Faust had chosen the easy way and had not suffered the experience of aging. Margurite had suffered, had endured the suffering, and thus destroyed the power of Mephistopheles. She destroyed the destroyer by her "suffering work."

That same salvation—that healing which is more than physical healing—was Edith's quest. The suffering work was the means of achieving it.

V

Before we leave Edith's experience and what it teaches us about suffering, I wish to lift up two tasks that are part of suffering work. They are the tasks of (1) working through the balance between separation and relation, and (2) working through the difference between identity and oneness. Without both tasks, the victory will not be won. Loss of the balance between identity and oneness, or separation and relation, results in either isolation or absorption. For Edith, however, the opportunity for new life and new opportunity made the task and the suffering not only worthwhile but essential.

One of the tasks in suffering is that of letting go—separation. The task has its problems at any age. Consider a person moving from home or school into the world. What a pleasure to be called a "promising young woman" or a "promising young man"! In those years, most of us have the structure of school or home to protect us. When the time comes to move into adulthoood, however, then we must "put away childish things" (I Cor. 13:11*c*). That "putting away" brings pain. Suffering work is the dynamic that deals with that pain.

Edith faced the same problem. Part of her work with the students, with her friends, with her failing body, and with me, was that of letting go. Separation requires the letting go of life as it is, in order to find a new relationship with life as it shall be.

Yet we need more than letting go. The other side of suffering work calls for taking up new relations. A young man and young woman, for example, must let go of their families upon moving into marriage. The work does not end with letting go of the past family. It also involves the task of taking up new relationships and working out a new family. That is not easy, for letting go means loss of the known, and new relations mean encountering the unknown. Nevertheless, when accomplished, the rewards are evident in all the benefits of maturity.

Thus, for Edith, the suffering work was evident not only in letting go, but in moving to a new dimension of life with a new way of thinking, of being herself. The development of the liturgy for the service of worship helped in that process. We may have some idea of what life is like after death, but no one is sure. However, part of the task for Edith came alive as she expressed a new relationship with God in preparing the service of worship.

To Edith's credit, she did not avoid the pain in the process of separation. She could have isolated herself, denied the feelings she was undergoing, lashed out at those who raised questions about what to do in the event of her death. Edith never denied the fact that we all live in relation to one another. The service of worship was the ultimate expression of affirming the nature of our relations.

The major religions differ on the matter of maintaining one's identity and maintaining oneness with others or with God. Eastern meditation sees the goal as moving into such oneness with the cosmos that all sense of identity is lost. The hope is that one ultimately moves off the wheel of karma into Nirvana, a blessed nonexistence. In fact, for some Eastern religions, to exist is the same as to suffer.

By contrast, in the Judeo-Christian understanding of suffering work, the task is not to lose one's identity, but to obtain oneness with God so as to gain one's identity. Edith found that struggle at the center of her experience. She rejected drugs in order not to lose her identity and her sense of oneness with God, and also to have the opportunity for reconciliation with those about her and with God. Thus, she discovered the new "being" that she was becoming. She had the capacity for loss which led to new discovery.

These tasks may also be seen at the level of faith, at the level of personal relationships, and at the level of internal feelings. At the level of faith, one needs to let go of earlier ideas about God in order to find God as God is. At the interpersonal level, loss of friends and relationships becomes a prerequisite for affirming those that are free and alive rather than compulsive and stifling. At the inner personal level, the willingness to lose one's soul leads to finding it. All these tasks were part of Edie's suffering struggle as she talked with me, thought about the words of Paul Tillich, and sensed her own dialogue with the God of Scripture.

VI

At this point, the story of Edith shows that care of a person who suffers calls for help in allowing a process that will:

1. affirm the sufferer in relation to God, to others, and to self;
2. find the balance between relation and privacy;
3. permit the suffering work.

Further, Edith's experience suggests that intellectual questions must decrease in favor of a relationship with God that gives meaning. This observation suggests an approach to the statement of John the Baptist: "I must decrease but he must increase." John raised questions about Jesus, and Jesus replied with examples of the effect of his relation to people, not with intellectual rational (John 3:30; Matt. 11:5). Chapter 6 returns to this point and speaks to the role of symbols in the task of suffering work. For the moment, note that developing the funeral plans themselves had a function for Edith—the function of finding those symbols that allowed the suffering work to come alive.

CHAPTER II

Biblical and Theological Views of Suffering

I define suffering work as the task of transforming the effect of pain from something that conquers us to something that we conquer. Suffering work is more than just dealing with evil. It is also the task of taking whatever touches our lives and "digesting" it so that that "whatever" becomes a part of us—a part of our healthy, living being.

We must not identify suffering work only with evil. When Jesus said, "Suffer the little children to come unto me," there was nothing evil about the children. Yet behind his statement is the need for all of us to integrate the young, the new, the vulnerable into the warp and woof of our lives.

"Suffering" is neither good nor bad. Suffering is necessary. It is the process by which we take the good or bad experience, the good or bad moment, and deal with it for the sake of health, wholeness, and salvation. Therefore, do not think of suffering only in regard to that which is bad. As in the case of a marriage, suffering work can be as beautiful as it can be painful. Marriage can be a beautiful experience, but that does not mean no adjustment, no change, no loss or pain.

Strangely, however, we are motivated more by what hurts than by what helps. Pain usually forces us to look for answers. Therefore the cases in Chapter 4 are primarily instances of tragedy or evil. Nevertheless, in some instances, note that we are dealing with healthy people or groups. There, the task of suffering work is to *maintain* health, not to *create* health. On other occasions, the task is to heal. In all cases, the task is to allow for creativity.

What affects us may be physical, mental-emotional, or spiritual. Just as we are familiar with solid, liquid, and gas forms, all of which have their own characteristics and needs, so there are different dimensions of suffering—physical suffering, mental-emotional suffering, spiritual suffering.

The Bible contains many examples of suffering and ministry to suffering. These examples may be looked at as case studies of suffering work. Generally, however, the authors did not present those studies in order to look at the psychological or physical dimensions of life. Rather, they were presented to illustrate that God was at work in them. The Bible bears witness to the way God works in our lives. The focus is on the spiritual dimension.

The biblical witness that suffering has a spiritual dimension (as well as psychological and physical) affects the way we look at these case studies. It is usual to analyze a case study as we would a laboratory experiment. We measure it, test it, analyze it. The case becomes an object. Yet, suffering is more than objective. Suffering has a spiritual dimension. And that dimension cannot be measured.

We can bear witness to a spiritual dimension.

We can experience a spiritual dimension.

We can gain understanding of a spiritual dimension and insight into it.

We cannot dissect and measure the spiritual dimension.

This may explain why the word *suffering* does not appear in the *American Dictionary of Psychoanalysis*. Neither does the word appear in the indexes of countless basic books on healing, counseling, and therapy. Suffering appears to be a basically biblical concept—a biblical contribution to our understanding of healing.

"Spiritual dimension" may mean different things to different people. For our purposes, I take our cue from the first chapters of Genesis. We read that we were created in God's image (1:27)—and therefore as creators; that God "breathed into his nostrils . . . and [he] became a living soul" (2:7). The spiritual dimension is the dimension of new creativity and the dimension of source-of-life in each of us.

Since creativity, by definition, means the bringing of something new out of nothing, it should be obvious that in suffering, we have something that cannot be measured, yet is real.

As we look at these case studies, then, we must view them differently from the way that has become traditional in the western scientific world. Carl Rogers, for example, would look at these cases on the basis of testing, for he holds that whatever exists, exists in a measureable form.[1] By contrast, we will look at these cases not just analytically, but *participatively*.

In looking at a study participatively, we will recognize the place of relationships in suffering. There is the relation of the sufferer to the life process that makes the suffering possible. There is also the relation to suffering of the person who witnesses suffering. In writing, the biblical authors became participants in the suffering. In reading these biblical and personal experiences, *we* become participants. We too suffer.

Therefore, our approach to these "cases" will not be to ask just what happened to this person, that group. We also will ask, "What happened to me?" I cannot tell you what that will mean for you as you read. I will tell you what happens to me. Yet you too must ask what happened to you as you viewed the story and became part of the suffering experience. Only then can you begin to know the meaning of suffering work.

I

Biblical studies are parables of suffering. In the examples, note the following:

1. In each instance, the problem is to find that which allows the suffering work to take place;
2. In each instance, the task is to find the symbols that will help put the suffering into context and also advance the process of the suffering work;
3. And in each instance, we are dealing with a creative process that results in a capacity to live creatively.

In line with reading participatively, I suggest that you read the episode, note how you feel after you have read it, and then go back to the episode to read again.

The first parable, in chapter 22 of Genesis, is the story usually called "the sacrifice of Isaac." We might better call it "the suffering work of Abraham."

Abraham hears God say to him, "Take your son, your only son Isaac, whom you love, and go to the land of Moriah, and offer him there as a burnt offering upon one of the mountains of which I shall tell you" (vs. 2). Abraham goes with his son, climbs the mountain, and prepares the fire. Isaac asks where the offering is, and Abraham says, "God will provide [an] offering" (vs. 8). When all is ready, Abraham binds Isaac and places him on the wood. Just as Abraham is about to sacrifice his son, he is distracted by a noise in the bush. There he sees a ram, senses it as God's provision for the sacrifice, frees Isaac, and sacrifices the ram instead.

Here the pain begins on a healthy level. Abraham is a healthy man, has a marriage that has survived many experiences, and has a fine son. Into this comes the pain that he must sacrifice his son, who is also healthy and whom he loves. As father and son go up the mountain, I sense a tremendous feeling of love and trust.

We have here a corporate experience—not just an individual experience. Abraham trusts God. Isaac trusts Abraham. The issue is not only what is happening to an individual—either Abraham or Isaac—but what is happening to them together.

In this corporate experience, we have a healthy trust. Abraham and Isaac do not need to be told that they need trust in order to survive in human relations. We do not need to be told that we need trust. The story assumes that need and reflects a healthy trust—a trust of each other and a trust of God.

Now comes a change: Abraham receives an order that shatters the view of God and the view of what it takes to be a good son. How can there be any meaning in a life that demands the sacrifice of a son . . . an only child? How can there be a God who allows this to happen? How can life make any sense when lived in this way? These questions and more are part of my struggle as I read the story.

Were these questions asked by Abraham, or by Isaac, or are they just ours? To some degree the questions belong to Abraham and Isaac, but not in the same way they are ours. Burnt offerings were known in those days. In some parts of the world, there was even human sacrifice—as even today remnants of such sacrifices to Kali continue in remote parts of India. Yet, Abraham is one whose awareness of God is growing. For Abraham, God is One with whom he can talk—even argue. Out of past experience, trusting God worked for Abraham—it got him out of Ur of the Chaldees, it got him out of Sodom, and it gave him a son in his old age. Therefore Abraham's approach may be different from ours; but surely there was questioning: Why? What did one make of this? Why a son in old age and now a command to sacrifice that son?

In reviewing the story, note that Abraham's suffering begins on what, in Edith's case, I called a cosmic level. His understanding of what it is to obey God and to love others comes into tension. We can imagine his prayer and meditation during the three-day journey. We can imagine his struggle to bring this tension into resolution.

Prayer is supposed to change things, but here it does not. Abraham goes through the suffering work. He trusts the process of that suffering work. He takes time to live with the situation, and he keeps alert for every clue that may help. He goes up the mountain. He prepares the fire. He trusts the process all the way. Suddenly, as he sees the ram, he finds the fruit of the suffering. He finds a symbol in the ram that gives him a new understanding of his relation to God and a creative way to express that relation in the future.

The pain, in this instance, appears at various levels. One level is focused on Abraham killing his own son. Another level centers on questioning the way he made sense out of faith. How painful to let go all that one has believed! The result was still faith in God, but faith understood in a more profound way than before. God appears to Abraham now in a newly expanded sense.

Abraham sought to deal with the pain. To handle the process of suffering work, he took the trip to Moriah. Out of the search for an adequate symbol, he saw the ram. Out of the experience, Abraham found a new sense of fullness and creativity. The remaining verses of the chapter reflect new horizons, hope, excitement. Oh, it may be possible to misuse the new creativity—it often was and it often is—but for the moment, the triumph was there.

From the perspective of biblical theology, the story of Abraham speaks to obedience as part of the life of faith. From the perspective of pastoral care, however, this case suggests a basic principle in suffering work: the gift of surrender.

The gift of surrender is the ability to let go. It is the ability to, as the apostle Paul said, "put in the past all that is in the past" (Phil. 2:13, paraphrased). Alcoholics Anonymous calls this the ability to let go and let God. Therein lies the ability to allow for death.

Suffering work is both the work of receiving this gift and the gift that makes the work possible. To the degree that we are learning to accept the need to surrender, we are involved in suffering work. Yet, to the degree that we do surrender, we allow the suffering work to heal us. The suffering work then carries us into a new level of our lives.

Abraham found the gift of surrender. Consider all he surrendered. He surrendered his ambition to have many descendents. He surrendered his emotional investment in his son. He surrendered his view of God—his view of everything that made sense out of life.

Yet, look at the results! The book of Romans says that this experience was "reckoned to him as righteousness" (4:3), meaning that Abraham found new levels of right relation to God, to his son, to himself. He still had God. Yet he had God, son, self, in a new way. Never again could he think of them as he had before. Now those relations had a deeper level of meaning than ever before.

All of us need this gift of surrender. The Abraham experience is not an isolated once-for-all event. When two parents put a child on the school bus for the first time, they sacrifice that child. When adult children find they must now care for their parents, they sacrifice the old relationships. When someone dies, we "surrender" that special someone to God. Out of the surrender, the parent finds a new experience with the growing child, the child with the aging parent, and all of us with a special someone now "with God."

Yes, this gift of surrender both comes through suffering work and makes suffering work possible.

The second parable is that of the Jews during the Exodus. Moses leads the Jews away from Pharaoh, but they do not go immediately into the Promised Land. Instead, they wander for forty years in the wilderness, eventually receive the law, and then are able to enter the Promised Land. However, many of those individuals who made the escape, including Moses the leader, do not enter the land. Only the *group,* as seen in the descendants of those who made the escape, is able to enter.

The book of Exodus shows that suffering work is necessary in corporate, or group, suffering, as well as in individual suffering. It also reveals that suffering work is part of a triumphant experience as well as a tragic one. The Jews were free! Liberation! Yet shortly, in the difficulties of the wilderness, they said that they might as well be back under Pharaoh. At least there, they had something to eat (chap. 17). As in the prior parable with the individual Abraham, now the whole body of people experience suffering that shatters the image they have of God.

In the wilderness and at the foot of the mountain, the people, as a people, search for a new symbol. Moses leaves them and goes up into the mountain to search for that symbol. He brings back an expression of their relation to the God who frees. The symbol that works is expressed in the words, "I am the Lord your God, who brought you out of the land of Egypt, out of the house of bondage"(20:2). In that context, there came the Ten Commandments.

However, the people, left to their own devices, build a symbol with their own hands—the golden calf. Out of their group struggle to find a symbol that is adequate, the suffering work becomes horrendous. People die. People are hurt. Finally, they are able to come to the mountain. Corporately, the old is let go and the the new symbol is found, as expressed in the Ten Commandments.

Out of the suffering work, the symbol has been found. The new creativity allows them to move on from Moses to Joshua, from Mount Sinai to the Promised Land.

Ask yourself again, "What is my own reaction as I read the story?" I sense the frustration of Moses. I can identify with the people's feeling—"Is it worth it?" I think of the blood-thirstiness in the story.

Yet, I also begin to feel the depth of the damage done to a people under oppression. They hated the oppressor, but the oppressor had become a part of their lives. They had not yet gained that freedom to live creatively. Pharaoh had become a part of them. It was necessary for that Pharaoh within them to die, just as did the Pharaoh behind them in Egypt. The forty years of wandering, the frustrations, the struggle, and the deaths reflect suffering work. The Exodus experience shows that this suffering work must take place in society as a whole, just as it took place in Abraham as an individual.

Upon analysis, then, what do we see?

Note that here again, Moses, as Abraham, not only must find the symbol, but allow for that suffering work whereby the group also finds the symbol. The suffering work resulted in letting go—not only of Egypt, but of a view of God that was no longer adequate. The *people* had to exchange an old sense of meaning for a new sense. It did not mean that there was no meaning or that there was no more suffering. It did mean that the new meaning allowed for the ability to cope with the suffering of the migration, the wars, the problems that would lie ahead.

The tasks of suffering work here, then, are those that allowed the people as a whole to sense their relation to the cosmic—the God who brought them out of the land of Egypt. It allowed them to sense the relation between love of God and love of neighbor.

As one traces the experience of the Jews, this pattern did not stop. The process of life is such that old meanings continually need to be let go and new meanings discovered. Inadequate symbols need to be released, and there must be the creativity of new symbols.

Here we have an introduction to the insights of the next chapter on developmental process. In the development of a people, old levels of life must be released and new ones found in the move from one life experience to another. Developmental psychology has shown that this ability is critical for personal growth; biblical study shows that this ability is equally important for the group.

In the instance of the Hebrews, new meanings were developed in that process. As time went on, the meanings were expressed through the writings of the Talmud and the Mishnah—documents in which rabbis worked out the application of the law to new and changing situations. These interpretations themselves then became a problem. The life and death of Christ may be looked at as a way, again, of seeking to meet that problem, allowing death and resurrection to be a part of daily life. Death and resurrection are the ultimate in the gift of surrender and the process of suffering work. However, we are getting ahead of ourselves.

In Job, we have yet another remarkable parable of suffering. Job loses everything. Bankruptcy, loss of family, physical illness, friends who do not understand him, demonstrate the depth of that loss. According to the story, he retrieves them—but not the same children and not the same wealth. Rather, there is a new understanding of God. When the new meaning comes clear for Job and all falls into place, he says, "I had heard of thee by the hearing of the ear, but now my eye sees thee" (42:5). That is to say, since we see things more clearly than we hear them, the suffering work allowed Job to see God in a deeper way than ever before.

In the story of Job, note also that that "sight" came while he was still in the midst of his suffering, not after he had regained his family. The return of the family, from the standpoint of the story, is a symbol of the new level that had been achieved.

The fourth parable from the Bible concerns Jesus and his disciples. The story is familiar. It must be seen in two parts—the part that relates to what happened to Jesus and the part that relates to what happened to the disciples.

Jesus is born and finds that he has a specific call. As he goes through his short life, a group of people—men and women, his disciples—become close to him. Jesus has great trust in the process of God, a trust so great that he allows a way of life that takes him to the cross.

As with Abraham, this cross is on one of the hills of Moriah. Unlike Abraham, the sacrifice is not relieved by finding an alternative symbol. Jesus himself—the son—becomes the sacrifice. He is his own symbol. As with Isaac, there are questions—but oh, the agony is seen at a far deeper level than in the other story! "Father . . . take away this cup from me," we hear Jesus say. Yet the trust of the process of God is complete: "Nevertheless, not what I will, but what thou wilt" (Mark 14:36). Again on the cross, we hear the question, "My God, why hast thou forsaken me?" (Mark 15:34). And again the agony, "I thirst" (John 19:28).

All accounts record the agony. How does it make you feel? Somehow, for me, at this stage of my life, I feel a profound sadness—a profound sense of identity with the depths of the struggle—a miraculous sense of being able to trust.

Two biblical writers—Luke and John—give us more of the agony than do the others. In those accounts, we learn that Jesus had a concern for those about him: "Father, forgive them" (Luke 23:34). . . . "To day shalt thou be with me in paradise" (Luke 23:43). . . . "Woman, behold thy son!" (John 19:26).

In those accounts we learn also that on the cross, Jesus achieved a sense of strength, peace, and resolution. "It is finished" (John 19:30) makes use of the Greek word *telios,* which suggests completion, wholeness. Everything has come together. "Father, into thy hands I commend my spirit" (Luke 23:46) suggests a new awareness of what it means to speak of God, to experience life, and to have the gift of surrender.

Do I correctly read what the experience meant to Jesus? Schillebeeckx reminds us that the Gospels are written out of the perspective and experience of the resurrection—however one interprets that experience.[2] It would be presumptuous for anyone to say definitively what the experience meant to Jesus. Yet certain observations are clear: Suffering for Jesus meant working through his relation to God and all that meant for him. Suffering was relational. For Jesus, suffering meant finding a new creativity—and symbols—for dealing with the event. Hence, the Haggadah of the Jews, celebrated on the Passover night, becomes reinterpreted by Jesus (as seen in the Gospels) and later by the disciples, in the sacrament of the Lord's Supper (as seen in both the Gospels and in the writings of Paul).

The triumph of this suffering work is expressed by the resurrection. The resurrection is the symbol that gives expression to the triumph and to the successful completion of the suffering work.

The passages also mean to me that the surrender to God means a surrender to victory. The victory may not appear at the moment, but the ultimate victory is assurred. Suffering work, we learn from this, has a goal. Suffering work is not just a matter of coping with a new experience—good or bad—but a time of achieving a victory to which we must surrender.

This aspect of surrender to victory has been lost in much of the emphasis on the crucifix and the sin of humankind. Many of us have been concerned that Christian Science, positive thinking, and "praise God" styles of faith miss the reality of life. Especially those of us who are professional care givers see so much of the tragedy of life that we are concerned about the dangers of denying the tragic. We feel that these approaches lead to that denial.

Yet there is a needed corrective in Unity, in Christian Science, in positive thinking, and in the moment of "praise God." Suffering work must involve not only working through the problem of a new stage in life, but surrendering to the solution when the problem is worked through. The symbols that allow for the "surrender to victory" are as important as the symbols of sacrifice that allow for letting go of the past. The gift of surrender, in suffering work, has as much to do with affirming our faith as with confessing our sin; with receiving God as with letting go of idols.

That brings us to the second part of the story—the disciples. The women find the empty tomb. The men and women disciples experience the empty tomb and, later, the presence of the resurrected Jesus. The disciples are told two things: Go into Jerusalem and stay there until you experience the Holy Spirit; then go out into the world and act on the experience you have had.

Although I take this report of the resurrection to be valid and the base of my faith, that is not the reason for looking at it here. Here, the purpose is to understand the process of suffering work as seen in the experience of the disciples.

At this point, I have difficulty in separating what I feel from what I believe the disciples felt. Surely there is a sense of confusion and failure (Peter denies Jesus and all scatter); surely there is a sense of emptiness; surely there is need for a deep inner healing that leads to the power for carrying on in life.

In studying the passages, however, does not the relational aspect of suffering work again emerge? The disciples must think of God in a new way, think of Jesus in a new way, think of one another in a new way. Jesus tells Mary not to touch him; that would be to grasp onto the old way (John 20:17). He tells her to act on what she knows—go tell the disciples. The disciples, in turn, are told to return to Jerusalem and stay there until the Holy Spirit comes upon them (Luke 24:49). Time for reflection, for inner healing, and for gaining the new power that comes whenever we "put it all together" becomes paramount.

In reviewing the experience of the disciples, we find in Jesus some beginning clues about the care giver in suffering work. Jesus was deeply aware of the place of relations and the need for a new creativity. His task was to help provide the structure that would allow for discovery of new relations. He was aware of the task of allowing for symbols that would permit a new creativity to come alive. From the readings in Schillebeeckx, we feel the Gospel writers also were aware of these needs.

The need for symbols to allow the relations to be experienced in a new way is seen in the instance of the disciples on the road to Emmaus (Luke 24:13 ff.). In that story, Jesus walks with the disciples but is unrecognized. Finally, in the breaking of bread, he comes alive to them. Their hearts "burned" and they sensed Christ in a manner different from their earlier way of thinking. The symbol allowed them to relate to the cosmos in a new way, and since they went back to see the other disciples, it presumably initiated relating to one another in a different way. Here there was a need for both conversation and action as a means of finding the right symbols.

Here, surrender to victory meant the need to let the old doubts and the old views die. Thomas (John 20:24 ff.) cannot put the new experience into the context of his old views. The presence of Jesus and the command to "put out your hand and place it in my side" breaks down all his old ways of thinking about Jesus. Thomas needed this new way of thinking, not only for his relations with Christ but also to restore his relations with the disciples. Otherwise, he would doubt them and they would resent his doubts. Until establishing his relation with Jesus, Thomas would have no peace with the group. Beyond that, moreover, peaceful relations with the disciples would express the newness of relations with Jesus.

(There is a temptation here to move into a discussion of what this means theologically. At the moment, however, we are not dealing with theology as such, but with the preface to theology—the actual experience. In this chapter, we will stay with the matter of the experience. Some of the theological implications will be discussed in Chapter 7.)

The disciples needed to make new for themselves the surrender to victory. The victory had to come alive. The solution was action. We often hear the command, "Go into all the world," as simply a statement to which we must be obedient. I believe that that interpretation misunderstands the dynamic. The need to "go forth" was not an arbitrary command to "speak the Word," but a statement of what was necessary to complete the process of suffering work. As one shares an experience with another, the reality of the experience then comes alive to the individual. As preparing the liturgy for her funeral helped Edith, witnessing would help the disciples.

We see an example of that truth in the musical *The King and I* when Anna sings, "By my students I am taught." We are taught not just because we can learn from one another. We are taught because, in the process of telling another what we know, we discover our knowledge with increased depth. Therefore, in acting on our faith, we discover what we in fact know. The healing becomes real. Elsewhere, I have called this realized forgiveness.[3] Here, I would call it realized victory.

Not just any action, however, can serve as the symbol. What works for a group may not work for a given individual. For example, as a group, the disciples are to cover all nations. As individuals, there is no such charge. On the contrary, there are numerous occasions when Jesus carried a person through the suffering work and then told the person to tell no one. On other occasions, such as the healing of one leper, Jesus made it clear that the telling must be specifically to certain individuals—the priests. Not just any act can be an effective symbol.

We have sound psychological basis for this limitation. When one talks too much about an experience, a problem called diffusion sets in. The experience begins to lose its depth as, like an overflowing river, it is spread all over the landscape. In fact, such spreading begins to make a god of the experience itself. This new god must also be surrendered.

The experience of surrender to victory must also be seen as part of a process—not the end of a process. The surrender to victory did not mean there would be no more suffering work. Life would go on. New experiences would need to be handled. There would be the reaction of the society to the new victory experienced by the new church. Suffering work does not end with the surrender to victory. Rather, the surrender simply sets the stage for the next process of suffering work, whatever that may be.

That surrender comes with the assurance that there are other victories to be experienced. As one matures in the victorious moments, the assurance becomes a hope—a hope that no matter how terrible the other moments of life, the process of suffering work will yet lead to new heights of victory.

To the lessons of suffering work learned from the story of Edith, we now add the lesson of surrender. The lesson has three parts:

a. surrender of the past to the past;
b. surrender to the victory of the present;
c. surrender to the expected hope of the future, based on the victory of the present.

Before we look at Chapter 4 to see how this discussion of "parables" from the Bible relates to practice, let us turn to the psychological dimensions of suffering in Chapter 3.

CHAPTER III

Psychological Dimensions of Suffering

From time to time in the opening chapters, I spoke of the needs of the suffering person. "Needs," however, can be ambiguous. What one person perceives as a need, another may not. In turning now to a brief look at the matter of needs, we must also remember to look at suffering in both corporate and personal dimensions.

Tragedy raises the question, Why? "How could God let this happen?" we ask. *When Bad Things Happen to Good People* becomes a title that sells a book.

As I have said, when properly understood, the real question is not, "Why did God let it happen?" but, "Where is God in all this suffering?" The question Why? is really a quest for meaning. We ask because we want to make sense of the tragedy. Once we make sense of it, we can cope with it. That insight alters the common understanding of what we need and of how to minister to a suffering person or group.

The need is for a sense of meaning. *Meaning* allows us to cope with suffering. At the moment one feels that God has not died or is not absent, one begins to sense that there must be a meaning; confidence in the reality of some meaning, somewhere, gives the ability to cope. That meaning leads us beyond the view that God does not care or that God is punishing us.

By way of example, a parishioner of mine was dying. He had incurable cancer. Often he would say, "I am sick and tired of being sick and tired."

On one occasion, he wanted to pray. After I had prayed with him, he said, "Lord, I do not know why I am still here. I have told you that I am quite ready to go. Still, I have to believe that there is some meaning in my being here. Is it in relationship to my family—to Jim here? Well, Lord, I would like to go, but if it is not time yet and you have a reason, I am content to stay."

The hope of some purpose, even though he really could not see it, was precisely what helped as this parishioner sought to cope with his dying, yet living.

In this chapter, then, we pause to look at three basic and helpful insights gained during the past thirty years. We ask, "How do these insights help with care of the suffering? And how does care of the suffering alter our view of these insights?"

One insight comes from the late Abraham Maslow.[1] He suggested that personal needs should be seen as a hierarchy. Another insight came from the work of Erik Erikson, but must be identified also with many other researchers (Freud, Goldstein, Jung, Gesell, Spock, to mention a few).[2] They suggested the concept of developmental stages in every life. The third insight came from Kurt Lewin and is associated with the view of field theory.[3]

I

In his view of the hierarchy of needs, Maslow encourages us to think of a pyramid. At the base of the pyramid are the fundamental needs. As one moves up, there are various levels. At each level, one finds new needs. As the needs at the lower levels are met, we move to the higher sets. Finally, at the top, are the most sophisticated needs.

At the first and *fundamental* level, all people have biological and physiological needs. For example, we need water. If we do not have water, we quickly die. All other needs are irrelevant, Maslow would say, if one is without water. One's view of politics or decision about what color to paint the ceiling make little difference to one who is dying of thirst in the desert. The same applies to the needs of food, air, shelter, sex, survival.

Maslow's identification of sex and survival as basic needs tells us something about needs—that needs are not always individual; they may also be social, or what I prefer to call corporate.

Consider sex. With regard to individual survival, the need for sex does not stand at the same level as the need for air. It does stand at the same level with regard to survival of the race. Without air, a person may die in moments. Despite jokes to the contrary, a person can go through a long life without a sexual experience. Without the expression of sex, however, what would die is the group—the race, the body of people. Maslow's identification of sex as a fundamental need, therefore, suggests that at the basic level, the corporate dimension of needs must be taken as seriously as the individual dimension. Sex assumes more than one person.

The need for survival teaches a similar lesson. We may speak of individual or group survival; we may speak of the survival of the person in the counseling room, the survival of the family, the company, the society, the world.

At the very foundation of the hierarchy of needs, therefore, we have evidence that the social/corporate dimension of suffering must be taken as seriously as the personal. We have fundamental evidence of our opening statement: We must not look at suffering from the standpoint of just the individual. There is group suffering.

Maslow calls the next level of needs *safety* needs. Needs for security, stability, dependency, protection; freedom from fear, anxiety, and chaos fit here. At this level, people find a need for structure, order, limits, guidelines. Structure allows for security and stability.

Some make the mistake of thinking that these higher levels of needs are less important than the lower ones. On the contrary, these needs, too, are life and death concerns. People can be literally "scared to death." The Bible opens with order coming out of chaos. (I call that the first great miracle—the miracle of structure, without which life could not exist.) People need structure for life and for coping with life. Its place on the pyramid does not change the critical nature of a need.

This truth has considerable importance when dealing with the suffering that accompanies change. Prisoners who have been released after a long time in jail may fall to pieces; the structure of the jail at least gave them security. A manager of a company in San Francisco had difficulty adjusting to a change in top management. He said to the new president, "Just tell me the rules. I can adjust as long as I know the rules of the game."

The difference between a higher and a lower level of need lies not in its importance for survival, but in its immediacy of importance. Obviously, if we cannot breathe, that need is more immediate than knowing the rules of the game. For a game to be played, however, the rules are fully as essential, ultimately, as the ability to breathe.

The third level of needs speaks to *love and belonging*. These needs find expression in love, affection, and group relations. The need for family or friends, a group or clan, is part of this level. The sense of community and community identity emerges here. The need for territorial rights becomes important—loyalty and patriotism are related at this level.

In identifying this level of need, Maslow himself lifted up the important dimension of the corporate in life. He also identified the fact that there is interaction among the levels. We do not deal with the first level and then finally move on to the second. Instead, the second or third may help us with the first.

This interrelation of the levels seems often to be missed. In the 1984 Olympics, a woman who was completing the marathon had become dehydrated. She could have stopped to receive help from the doctors. However, the presence of the crowd suggested another way to solve the problem.

This second way was to deal with her group need. There would have come a time when the dehydration would have taken over. Until that time, the runner could choose one of two approaches—group support, or water from the doctors. She chose the former. The sense of the group support and of the attendants running with her carried her through to the end. She finished the race, and then attended to the issue of water.

Fortunately, the woman judged her biological ability correctly. By the same token, she gave evidence that she could deal with the biological state—at least up to a point—from a high level on the hierarchy of needs.

Or consider the matter of the need for water among runners who did not face collapse. While racing, they were aided by spectators who ran out to them with water. The fellowship of the group made that aid possible. The creation of the group becomes, in those instances, the means of dealing with the biological problem.

Sadly, we often see the reverse of that process. When a bus driver in San Francisco was attacked, the riders (the members of the group) rushed off the bus and left the driver to his fate. In effect, those on the bus looked at the pain and chose not to suffer. Without the group, the driver had no source of help for even his "lower" level of needs. (Happily, at least one of the group on the bus later chose to suffer. A woman returned to help the injured driver. The willingness of the group to suffer, limited as it was, proved basic to survival.)

Maslow moves on in his hierarchy of needs. Almost at the top, he speaks of the *esteem* needs. Self-esteem, esteem from others, a sense of achievement and recognition from others, self-confidence and mastery of the environment, are important.

Elie Wiesel, in *Night,* his story of the Holocaust, writes that after the liberation, he and others went through the town near the concentration camp and did not feel revenge. Why? In part, they felt no revenge because they had survived—and that was more important than revenge. They had their self-esteem. Revenge would have betrayed that self-esteem. Revenge would have meant descending to the level of those who put them through the horror. As with Edith, their suffering had allowed them to maintain their integrity and their esteem. Later, the cry for justice would bring about the effort to punish war criminals. For the moment, their concern was personal esteem—recognition that they had triumphed in the midst of the horror.

Finally, there comes what Dr. Maslow calls the need for *self-actualization*—a sense of directing one's own life—and that need has at its center the desire for meaning and purpose.

At this point, the understanding of suffering work requires a new look at Maslow. Also at this point, I must disagree with an implication of Dorothee Söelle in her remarkable and excellent book *Suffering*, and with Rabbi Kushner in his popular and readable *When Bad Things Happen to Good People*. Maslow considers *meaning* the last of the needs. Söelle implies that it is the loss of meaning that leads to the sense of suffering.[4] Rabbi Kushner feels that the idea of purpose is a nice thought, but unrealistic at worst, and at best, not sufficient.[5]

On the contrary, the sense of meaning is precisely what allows one to cope with suffering and to deal even with the loss of air. The biological needs are indeed necessary. Yet, what helps us deal with biological needs? For Edith, wrestling through the sense of meaning freed her to deal with the impending loss of breath. The sense of meaning allows one to cope with suffering. As identified before, the "higher" needs may be critical for dealing with lower needs.

This truth is caught by Archibald MacLeish in his epic poem *J. B.*, based on the book of Job.[6] In a striking moment, the play portrays Job sitting on his dung heap. Job chooses to suffer. His wife says to him, "Curse God and die." She holds that his faith is worth nothing. Everything is wrong with the faith. In the course of the argument, Job cries out, "It does not mean there is no meaning." Job is still on his dung heap, remember, when he receives his sense of meaning! True, lack of meaning increases suffering, and its presence does not end suffering. Yet, even awareness that meaning exists—though still undefined—allows us to cope with the dung heaps in our lives.

If my observation on suffering is correct, the hierarchy of needs must not be looked at as an orderly sequence of tasks to be accomplished. We do not move from the first to the second to the third levels in neat order. Rather, we move back and forth in a dynamic interaction of levels. This back-and-forth action makes the process of suffering work complex in both theory and practice, just as the process of development is complex.

The picture Maslow has given us helps; but another picture may help even more in suggesting the complexity. The picture must be seen not so much as a pyramid as a spiral of needs that act and interact. When we stand at the top of a spiral staircase, we can look down and see all the levels at once. A wire spiral can be compacted so that the last part of the spiral lies on the same place as the first. It can be pulled out so that the first part is truly first.[7]

If one accepts the spiral as a metaphor, a different sense of the relationship of needs emerges from that in the pyramid. In the spiral, needs are like places that move in and out of relation to one another. Sometimes one comes before another, and at times all are on the same level.

Those of us who would help in the matter of suffering work must have the flexibility to move with the spiral. We must be prepared to give air when air is needed and to help with the sense of meaning when the sense of meaning is the issue. The moment of prayer may enable the sufferer to be open enough to receive the water. The water may revive the sufferer enough to find the moment of meaning. The spiral of needs thus expands and contracts. One thing it does not do: It does not go away.

II

The hierarchy-of-needs metaphor proves helpful; but the hierarchy must also be seen in relation to what we know from developmental psychology. This teaches us that there are stages in life; that at each stage, there are tasks we must accomplish. Suffering work is the work of going through the pain of each task at each stage.

The example of developmental stages comes from studies done years ago.[8] In those studies, polliwogs were watched. The researchers noted that a polliwog first learns to swim by making a slight random movement with the tail. It then learns to make the tail form a slight curve. From the curve, the polliwog moves to making the tail into an S shape. Finally, the tail wiggles.

At no time does a polliwog move from the slight random motion to the fast wiggle. Each stage is followed. One polliwog may go through the stages faster than another, but no stage is missed totally. The task is to master each stage in order to have a foundation for moving on the the next stage.

The move from one stage to another—leaving the familiar and moving to the unfamiliar—carries its share of pain, pain experienced as loss. Yet if the polliwog likes the curved-tail level of life and will not move to a higher level, it will never learn to swim.

In life, unfortunately, some of us become so comfortable with the stage we are in that we choose not to leave it—we choose not to suffer. We choose to protect ourselves against pain by staying where we are. The resultant arrested development, or stagnation, or death, illustrates the impossibility of life without the developmental process. The suffering work that allows for that process must be chosen.

We humans are not polliwogs, but the lesson applies. An individual or a people may choose to stay at one level of the hierarchy of needs and not move on. Food is a basic need. It would be possible—and did happen in the concentration camps—that a person would wallow in the matter of obtaining bread. He or she would not deal with other areas on the spiral of needs or stages of development. Those of us who were not there but have seen suffering or have had a taste of it, can fully understand the emotion of one who "wallows" at the level of seeking bread. Yet the miracle is that many did not stay at that level. The reports of Anne Frank, Elie Wiesel, and others, demonstrate that miracle. They endured the suffering work—often through their writings—and maintained a wholeness of life that was not destroyed by the evil.

People may also regress. A person or group may move back to a prior level. In sickness, for example, others care for one who is sick, and the person experiences care as comforting. As one recovers, how tempting it is to hold on to the moments of being pampered. Every nurse on a hospital ward knows that there comes a time when a patient must be weaned from "nursing," even as an infant must be taken from its mother's breast. The pain may not be pleasant. Nevertheless, the suffering work allows one to move back out of the time of regression into maturity. That suffering work has the task of letting go the infant stage to which one had retreated as a patient.

Be aware of the difference between *stages* as discussed here, and *needs* as presented by Maslow. Stages relate to maturity; needs, to survival. A person may be of legal age in chronological years, yet not act with maturity. Age does not guarantee maturity.

However, maturity itself must be carefully defined. In the field of developmental psychology, maturity is seen as the capacity to fulfill oneself at whatever stage of life one happens to be. Maturity is related to the Christian word *perfect*. When Jesus said that we were to be perfect, the word he used would be better translated *whole*. To be whole, at whatever stage of life, is to be mature.

This definition makes us rethink our basis of understanding maturity. People will look at a child who can play a Bach fugue and say, "My, how mature!" That child is not mature; that child is precocious. Maturity means being what we are at the stage of life where we are. In the developmental definition, a child who can handle the *inability* to play a Bach fugue, when indeed that is not a natural talent, shows maturity. That child has developed fully for that stage of life and thus meets this definition of maturity. For all people, the developmental definition of maturity therefore separates maturity and the meeting of needs. Jesus on the cross did not have all his needs met. Yet his actions demonstrated wholeness. In the midst of a complex of needs, including the need for water, Jesus was a mature man.

When it comes to caring in the suffering moment, we need, then, to identify the issue. Survival may be the issue; or maturity may be the problem; or a combination of both may be involved. We must not confuse healing with only the issue of survival. Even death may demonstrate maturity. We will return to this point in the next chapter.

III

To Maslow's hierarchy of needs and the subject of developmental stages, we add the concept of *field theory*.

According to field theory, we are not people in isolation—we all are parts of a field of interacting experiences and personalities. When we sit in a room alone, we have a relationship with the walls, the quiet, the view out the window. Let one person enter that room, and everything changes. Where once we were alone, now we share a relation with another soul. The surroundings are the same; the dynamic has changed. Add a third person: more change; for each additional person: more change.

Field theory requires us to consider seriously the corporate aspect of suffering. Those of us who would bring healing, who would intervene, must sense the "field" in which suffering takes place. Otherwise we deal only with symptoms and not with root causes. (In a later chapter, we will see that this field affects us as healers and is affected by us. We will see that we suffer and are drained, we heal and are healed.)

In the late 1960s, the Community Service Society (CSS) of New York developed this awareness of the corporate side of suffering in the matter of intervention.[9] In conducting a major survey of New York City, CSS observed that problems do not arise in isolation. Rather, they are always in clusters. To meet a certain problem, those who would heal must be aware of and deal with the cluster. Apart from the cluster, a particular issue might be met, but only temporarily. As it were, the illness might be cured, but not the patient.

One instance concerned a hotel on the west side of Manhattan near the Museum of Natural History. Statistics showed a high rate of suicide in the area. Statistics also showed a high rate of drug abuse. "Obviously," since both suicide and drugs are prevalent among teenagers, something needed to be done for the young people.

Wrong!

What seemed obvious was not the case. The cluster study showed that the area also had a high instance of SROs (single room occupancy). In that part of the city, many single rooms housed either families or single individuals. Especially in the instance of the single individuals, many were elderly and many were from Puerto Rico. A look at the cluster gave a new sense of the emotional dynamics in that hotel and among those people. There, our social workers dealt with people who needed to survive in a strange land. Many of those elderly people did not want to give up the battle. Yet, to live alone in a single room, isolated from others, was an adjustment for people accustomed to the warmth of the Spanish casa (home).

Those people, as a people and as individuals, were vulnerable to drug hustlers. With drugs, suffering work could be avoided. When drugs proved insufficient, suicide looked inviting. Suicide was the ultimate escape from the suffering work. And why not? For people in that condition, the process of the suffering work itself seemed beyond them. They needed the opportunity of suffering work, help in identifying the task of suffering work, and the means for carrying out the task.

As a result, when drugs were not enough or out of reach, suicide was the remaining avenue. Contrary to national statistics, in this area the high suicide rate was among the elderly—not the youth.

Help, then, required intervention at all areas—loneliness, aging, drugs, depression, culture. Since a field is a system of relations, feelings, and issues—all of which impinge on one another—intervention meant attention to each of these areas. They are not isolated, with no relation to the others.

In the instance of New York, the Community Service Society targeted specific hotels with SROs. In those hotels, CSS established opportunities for people to meet and socialize. It created tenant training and intergenerational programs, opportunities for adult education and individual counseling. Thus CSS sought to bring help by allowing for suffering work to take place in the whole cluster.

IV

Corporate suffering itself has certain needs that can be lifted up and put beside Maslow's discussion, the insights of developmental psychology, and the knowledge of field theory. Case studies of corporate and individual suffering will be reviewed in the next chapter. Here, it is sufficient to focus on the interplay of forces in any group and ask, "What does it take for a group to survive?"

Studies of the family, of group dynamics, of interpersonal relations, can lead to a long list of needs for group survival, but I would identify three: togetherness, support, identity. In order to meet these needs, there must also be a balance in the group of trust, judgment, and respect.

As one reads story after story of people who went to Dachau or other prison camps, the sense of needing to be with someone is clear. I recall a report that Anne Frank was last seen holding the hand of her younger sister as they walked together, possibly to the gas chamber. The fact that prisons regard solitary confinement as an ultimate punishment and seek to depersonalize individuals by giving them numbers, shows that a sense of personhood requires both identity and relations with others. People in concentration camps were given numbers and treated in ways that depersonalized them. To fight depersonalization, those incarcerated did little things to establish a sense of the personal and maintain relations with one another.

Similarly, a psychiatric patient in a Canadian hospital made a friend of a mouse; a prisoner at Alcatraz became interested in birds. In case after case, a deep instinct seeks to give a sense of relationship—of togetherness. Out of that sense of togetherness comes a need for support, for without support, a group soon disintegrates and everyone becomes defensive. The sharing of ends, the healing, and the ability to look creatively at problems simply evaporates.

Thus Scripture continually refers to the people of God—not just to individuals. A people that knows it belongs—especially that it belongs to God—becomes strong, creative, and able to cope. In the Bible, "belonging to God" expresses itself through being forgiven, being led into the land of milk and honey, and achieving victory over evil. The suffering work of a group is that group's ability to experience the sense of belonging that allows for personal victory during a time of evil.

The story of Gideon and a small group attacking the walls of Jericho, the story of a people taking a new leader after Moses died, the story of a people having a Redeemer—all are instances of a capacity for group support leading to a new life.

The group also needs a focus that gives it identity. This focus may be the flag, a leader, a creed, a faith, or a tragedy. In days of ancient battles, the flag identified the leader and thus held the group together. The people knew who gave them identity. In the Presbyterian Church, the *Book of Confessions* begins with the great creeds of the church. After we had experimented in my parish with different modern creeds, a woman said, "Please bring back the Apostles' Creed; I want to know that I belong to the historic church." A similar effect comes at the time of a national tragedy such as an invasion or the death of a well-loved personality. The death of a father may bring together separated children who, in that death, rediscover their identity with one another. The death of a national leader often has the same effect.

In some organizations there has been an emphasis—usually associated with the thinking of psychologist Carl Rogers—on leaderless groups. Yet even in such groups, the reality is never lack of leadership as much as shifts in leadership. First one person will assume the role, and then another. What the "leaderless group" really teaches proves contrary to the claims of the advocates of such groups. Rather than the absence of a leader, the group receives its identity from more than one leader. An event—a war won, a friend dying, a couple being married, a ship sinking—may take an assortment of individuals and make them a group. In the case of a spouse, a school, a business, or a country, people may choose their group. In a tragedy such as an earthquake, the collapse of a building, a mass killing, strangers suddenly find themselves part of a group they did not choose. More is involved than one leader, but leaders emerge.

These three needs alone—togetherness, support, identity—do not guarantee group survival. The group also needs a process. The process must be marked by trust, commitment, and justice. Without these, no group will last. (This is not to say that individuals do not also need trust, commitment, justice. It is to say that the studies of processes that allow individuals to develop must have their parallels in processes that allow groups to grow and mature.) Trust is necessary, because trust leads to the capacity for love and the opportunity for communication. I define trust as *the capacity for vulnerability in the presence of another.* Without such trust, we cannot receive what others offer us. Without trust, we will not risk offering anything of ourselves to others.

We must also have commitment, for without commitment we cannot believe that the trust will be there—or that the risk will be worth taking. In the marriage service, for example, we do not ask whether the two people love each other. Rather, we ask whether they *will* love each other—will commit themselves to loving each other. Without that commitment, there is no chance that the relationship will survive. Similarly, for group survival, a group needs commitment from its various elements.

Justice, too, is critical for group survival. Without justice (the dimension of rightness), trust will not survive. Justice provides the structure that protects the vulnerability of trust. The Danish thinker Sören Kierkegaard has written most helpfully on this point. His essay on the relation between justice and love suggests that trust without justice is mere romance; and justice without trust becomes tyranny. Justice establishes the kind of rules and structures by which a group can know how to relate. Justice gives some guarantee as to the rules within which one may operate.

The structure of justice is not the same for all groups. Each culture has its own. Each family develops its own. Some structures are adequate and some are not. The task in helping some groups deal with suffering is the task of helping to build an adequate structure of justice.

The point here is not to determine an appropriate trust and an adequate structure. The point here is that both are needed. From the Christian standpoint, the purpose of trust and structure is healing. Justice is not a matter of revenge, not a matter of repayment to society, but a matter of redemption.

V

Before concluding this chapter, I wish to say a few words about scapegoating. In the next chapters, we will consider appropriate ways of dealing with suffering work. Scapegoating is an inappropriate way that is tried all too often; it harms others and also fails suffering work. As care givers and as people who suffer, we need to understand the dangerous dynamic of scapegoating.

Whether in the life of a group or an individual, scapegoating is an attempt to find a reason for pain. It is a means of trying to deal with suffering. Scapegoating is a way of saying, "Our group can identify the problem of our pain by blaming someone. That allows us to make sense (meaning) out of the pain and deal with it."

Scapegoating equals ineffective suffering work. Scapegoating deals with pain, but deals with it in a way that avoids responsibility for the pain or for the task of working it through.

In common parlance, we do not understand the function of scapegoating. Most of us think of it as simply blaming someone else for our troubles. Scapegoating is that—but it is more than that. The term comes from the days when a tribe would gather and place a goat in the midst of the people. Each member of the community would lay a hand on the goat—symbolically placing his or her sins on the animal. When the ritual was finished, the goat would be pushed into the wilderness of the night. In that way, all the sins and failures of the community were eliminated. The act was seen as an act of healing for the community. Scapegoating became a form of suffering work because it allowed for dealing with pain.

In time, people began to sacrifice goats in religious rituals. In the Bible, there are various kinds of goat offerings—thank offerings, peace offerings, sin offerings. To the idea of sins being carried away in the death of the goat, there then was added the idea of paying a god. The god would be placated by offering the goat.

The Judeo-Christian faith moved beyond the idea that God needed to be placated. The prophets spoke of God wanting not sacrifice but justice and mercy. In so-called Christian countries, we think we have moved beyond scapegoating as an appropriate practice, but unfortunately, we have not. Hitler blamed the Jews by making them the scapegoat for the problems of the world. A family turns on a child as the scapegoat for all that happens. A player in the World Series misses a ground ball and becomes the "goat" for the team's loss. Children blame a father or mother not only for their problems but for the way in which they deal with their problems.

In corporate suffering, we must become aware of the need to which scapegoating points and of the danger in it. Only then will we move beyond the practice.

Scapegoating points to the need for being cleansed, the need for healing; it points to the need for commitment to deal with that which causes pain—and to deal with it in a way that does not avoid responsibility. The danger of scapegoating lies in placing the responsibility for the pain on one person or group. The awareness of personal sin or failure, the need for suffering work, then is avoided, and destruction follows—destruction of the person who is made the goat and destruction of the group that avoided the suffering work.

The healer, in dealing with corporate suffering, must help the group become aware of scapegoating.

Those in the group must see that scapegoating destroys trust, avoids commitment, and removes any structure that will allow the group to survive. After all, if one person can become the scapegoat, when that person leaves (as ultimately all scapegoats must), who will be next? Any structure on which members of the group can count is lost.

That phenomenon shows up again and again. An alcoholic who becomes violent may attack his wife. If the wife leaves, the attack moves to the children as a target . . . or his job, or his friends. If a controversial figure dies or leaves, those who "hated" that person find another to hate. As a pastor, for example, I have found that those in a parish who were unhappy with my predecessor will ultimately be unhappy with me. In each case, the scapegoat becomes part of the life of those who are scapegoating. When one goat leaves, another must be found.

Scapegoating demonstrates that the members of a group have not succeeded in lifting up the failure or sin or anger that is theirs. For a while, scapegoating protects the group against pain and seems successful. Therefore, we resist looking at the scapegoating function in ourselves or others. Only when the situation becomes so bad that people must look beyond scapegoating will the group begin to recognize this destructive means of dealing with suffering. Unfortunately, such recognition often comes too late to avoid real damage.

The helper, then, needs to direct the group to see what the scapegoating may represent. The group may need to be aware of its sin, of that which needs to be atoned. Perhaps the group needs to see the scapegoating as a search for meaning in a time of pain.

Often in the process of the search, God becomes the scapegoat! How often and how subtly, God, to whom we once offered the sacrifice, becomes the sacrifice. "God must be punishing me" or "It is God's will" represent two attempts to put the blame on God. Even "This is a test of faith" may be a form of scapegoating, a way of putting the responsibility on God—the suffering is that intense.

Yet all these comments basically show our need for meaning—our need for a way to make sense out of suffering in order to cope with it. And all these forms of scapegoating become means of avoiding the suffering work by both a generalization about God and an assumption. The generalization is that everything we are experiencing in pain can be seen as punishment. There are indeed consequences of sin; however, not all that happens is a consequence of "our" sin. When the people asked whether it was the man blind from birth or his parents who had sinned, Jesus' answer was "neither." Generalization that results in blaming God for our pain or in claiming that all pain is God's punishment for our sin actually avoids suffering work. Such scapegoating of God avoids the suffering work of sorting out the different aspects of pain and the different meanings around pain.

We may be the innocent victims of sin. To blame God for punishing our sin is to forget something about God and about ourselves. It is a way of forgetting that God loves; it is to forget that, in fact, we may do some things right. The first view makes God too small; the second makes us too small.

Scapegoating God assumes that we really can know God's mind. Such scapegoating puts us on the level of God because we can assume that we know what God is doing. Whether in the individual or the group, part of the approach to suffering is the awareness that we indeed cannot know all the answers. We are not all-knowing.

The use of a scapegoat, then, seeks to provide meaning by saying that we are not responsible. The process of healing requires that suffering work through which the individual or the group can look at the pain, accept the responsibility, and decide upon appropriate ways for dealing with that pain.

VI

If, then, scapegoating is not the answer, if a sense of meaning is important for both the individual and the group, what does the Christian faith have to bring to the suffering moment?

The Christian faith may suggest some answers to the question usually asked, "Why did God let this happen?" but the response points in another direction. If we deal with suffering through the issue of meaning, the question becomes, "Where is God in this?" To that question, the Christian faith responds.

The response, best expressed in a story from Elie Wiesel's *Night*, is a helpful model. Wiesel speaks of being in the concentration camp. Three victims were to be executed by hanging. Two were adults. One was a child. The adults died quickly. The child, because of light weight, died slowly. The prisoners were required to walk past the sight. As they trudged past, someone in the group asked, "Where is God now?" Deep inside himself, said Wiesel, there came a voice: "Where is He? Here He is—He is hanging here on this gallows."[10]

Where is God? God is in the suffering.

Because of the tragic flaw of freedom and responsibility, there is and shall be evil in the world. God has not abandoned the world. God is in the world—even in the suffering. In the suffering, God seeks to work out the purposes of love. The process hurts, but in the suffering work, God works! Out if it comes a healing of the soul—the soul of the individual and the soul of the group. That lesson, we saw in Edith. That truth became Job's insight.

Some say God can do everything. They criticize when they do not feel there is sufficient emphasis placed on the healing prayer. "God heals," they say.

Yes, God heals. But what God heals is the damage done by evil and the presence of evil itself. God will not do that by becoming evil. God will not do that by healing the body at the expense of the soul—including the body of a group. God will not do that even to keep us happy—those of us who believe. There is a place for the healing prayer. However, there is never a place for a healing prayer that would rob God or us of the ultimate healing—the healing of all evil!

This observation has a practical application. Those who pray for healing will pray until the person has died. Yet, if the ultimate healing is the healing of all evil, should not the prayer continue?

In the Roman Catholic tradition, there is a sacrament for the sick, formerly called extreme unction—literally meaning *extreme anointing.* The rite can be given when a person is seriously ill or facing serious surgery, but is most commonly given when someone is thought to be near death. Protestants generally have rejected this rite, either because they consider it magical or because they do not hold it to be a sacrament. Roman Catholics do not reject it totally, yet many I know do not seem to understand its meaning. Moreover, people do not understand its legitimate place in relation to suffering.

One meaning of penance refers to the preparation of the soul for death, and one way of expressing that preparation is the act of extreme unction. The rite of extreme unction recognized that the battle did not end with death, that this suffering was and is not an isolated instance. Rather, the suffering was and is part of the bigger battle against the forces of evil. The victory was won on the cross, but the fulfillment of that victory has yet to be completed. As the Scripture says, the last enemy to be defeated will be death itself (I Cor. 15:26).

Thus, the need for cosmic healing continues. The person who died was and still is part of that cosmic experience. Extreme unction recognized that experience.

In this sense of recognition, we need to build on the lessons of extreme unction for help with the moment of suffering. The healing prayer is as appropriate after death as before. Shakespeare expressed it positively when Horatio said at Hamlet's death, may "flights of angels sing thee to thy rest." In our ministry, we too must find that positive expression.

What, then, is appropriate to suffering work and to the healer who would intervene and help in the suffering moment? The appropriate begins with a genuine awareness of the presence of evil in the world. The demonic is real.

In this chapter, I have raised the matter of group, or corporate, suffering. Awareness of that suffering is important—not just because we are parts of groups, or because there is such a thing as group suffering. Awareness of corporate suffering is important because we are all part of that group known as humanity. As such, we all are part of the process of God's battle with evil.

The reality of evil must be clear if we are to deal with suffering either in our understanding or in our ministering. Not to sense that individual suffering is itself a part of cosmic corporate suffering—corporate suffering on a grand scale—is to reduce the scope of the battle. Aware that we form part of the battleground against evil on a cosmic scale, we then can think through approaches, interventions, that deal with the full aspect of the battle. When we know not only that our God is not too small, but that our sense of evil is not too small, we begin to have an adequate response to the suffering around us. We cannot have a workable solution if we do not properly read the issue.

With this background, we now turn to several case studies. In these studies we seek to find how, in fact, ministry to those who suffer can help. We shall try to lift up helpful and unhelpful ministries. We ask, "What may we legitimately expect by way of our approach to the healing moment of suffering and what we call suffering work?"

CHAPTER IV

Contemporary Views of Suffering

Corporate Suffering

We have said that the Christian faith turns to the question, "What meaning helps me deal with what is happening to me?"

Care givers deal with pain. The person who hurts deals with the hurts, the problems. Until recently, most of the initial books on suffering centered on one-to-one counseling. Especially among ministerial types, the individual was the focus.

Over the past few years, the knowledge of systems and groups has led to awareness of group and family counseling. Dorothee Sölle's book *Suffering* has moved beyond the group to the full arena of corporate, or societal, suffering. She looks at the suffering of people in the Holocaust and again in Vietnam. Social work approaches since World War II have further helped this shift. Community organization and community organizers, public policy studies and public policy specialists, have developed a strong base during these years. Group therapy itself indicates a difference between dealing with the individual alone and the individual in a group.

Various approaches to therapy have developed in relation to systems theory, to transactions between individuals or among groups, to interpersonal theories. Although I am not reviewing those theories here, they form the background for much of what is said. Study of those theories will benefit readers not already familiar with them.

Other approaches to suffering center on structure. The organization of a city, a business, a culture, either helps minister to suffering or hinders the suffering process. Countries that do nothing about shanty towns, open sewers, and poor health structures hinder the approach to suffering. In the United States, churches that believe they have the right to give sanctuary to any individual who has a need find themselves in conflict with governments that oppose individuals entering from a country such as El Salvador. The conflict centers on the legal and political structures required to deal with suffering, as well as on whose suffering will be heard—the suffering of those in our nation, the suffering of the wider community of human beings, or both.

In this chapter, the approach to corporate suffering centers on the concept of clusters. In any community, helpers must identify the clusters of problems and the systems of clusters that bear on an individual or on a group of individuals. If any real ministry to suffering takes place, it will come only because the nature of the clusters has been identified and understood by the church, the social service agency, or the individual who deals with suffering.

Long before modern social scientists, the Bible addressed questions of community process and structure. The Ten Commandments gave a structure not only for individual life but for a whole society. A community such as Qumran near the Dead Sea established a structure for dealing with social, personal, and religious issues. The Sermon on the Mount and the early church called for a set of structures that changed the whole approach to living.

The servant model of leadership given by Jesus revolutionized the concept of management. That approach overthrew the pyramid model. In the pyramid model, the manager at the top rules or delegates. In the Jesus model, the manager does not take too seriously the place at the top, often yields to the person on the "bottom," and serves rather than rules.

In the Christian world based on Scripture, the question of structure becomes a question of love and stewardship. How shall we oversee the earth for which Adam has responsibility? We must care for that which has been entrusted to us—not see it as merely an opportunity for profit or self-aggrandizement.

For an example of both the cluster and the stewardship approach to corporate suffering, consider again the Community Service Society's study of New York City. In the early 1970s, the CSS studied that city to find the needs to which the agency should respond. The research looked at every health district within the city and identified problems of culture, problems of economics and housing, and problems of special need. Twenty-two key concerns emerged, such as suicide, aging, drug use, teenage pregnancy, arrest, overcrowding.

As the study proceeded, the researchers discovered that in any given area, no problem occurred alone. All problems were part of a system—part of a cluster of problems. Further, all problems were found to have different meanings in different cultures. The drug problem in a primarily Spanish-speaking area had different aspects from the same difficulty in a primarily black area. And both were different from a drug problem in a white area. To move into an area of poverty and deal with the hurt, the pain, and the suffering required attention to the cluster, not just to the individual.

In the following cases, the fundamental question centered on how best the church or the agency could bring its resources to bear on the problem so that real change could took place and real pain end. Those resources were individual, political, social, economic, spiritual. The problem was the stewardship of the individual lives of the care givers and of those who needed the care. The solution rested not in great pronouncements, but in seeking to serve through the most effective means possible.

Given that background, we now consider examples of suffering work in corporate settings. I suggest that each be read for the general feel. Identify that feeling as you read, then look at the commentary.

A. The South Bronx section of New York City is one of the most depressed areas in the country. In the late 1960s, it was so depressed that riots did not even occur. Instead, the police were called three and four times a day for a crime, a death, an unexplained fire.

A study of the area indicated a cluster of poor housing, crime, murder, drugs, unemployment. The area was primarily Puerto Rican. The group had little mobility; any that existed meant only moving from place to place within the area.

A coalition of a private builder, a social service agency (the Community Service Society), and city and state agencies established a program. They built new apartments that would house ten thousand people. The funding came from the government, the apartments were built privately, and a counselor worked with the people. At the outset, the builder employed the social worker. After occupancy, CSS took over.

During the time the land was being razed and the building established, the agency and the builder identified the community inhabitants. Through this identification, the leadership established a process and guidelines for renting the new space. Eighty percent of the tenants were to be people originally from the area. All were interviewed and asked to agree to membership in the tenant organization. Within the tenant group, standards were established. The tenants decided to police their own property. After dialogue among the tenant, management, and social work groups, educational programs were established. In these programs, the tenants looked at their own culture. They thought through the differences between living in Puerto Rico and living in the Bronx. Basic matters were explained (e.g., "The toilets will not handle garbage; we do not throw garbage out the window.").

Upon occupancy of the completed buildings, the social service staff included two professional social workers with counseling skills, seven community people trained in social work, and a community-based support staff. The social service agency, CSS, ran this program. During the first ten months after occupancy, there was one murder. (Larchmont, New York, a wealthy suburb in Westchester County with the same number of people, also reported one murder during that same time!)

The revolution that took place may be called minor. Yet, revolution did take place—a revolution in the whole approach to dealing with people in economic and social pain. This experiment represents good stewardship—making the best use of human, physical, and political resources. It also represents an example of suffering work at the level of a group of people, not just an individual. Consider what happened:

In the first place, people decided to endure the suffering of the community rather than run away. People in business, government, and social work "stuck with it," and people in the community did not give up. Those who intervened brought not only resources but a sense of hope. The establishment of trust and the coming of people who had a power base bought hope.

Further, power was shared in two directions. As the social workers arrived and gained trust, they began to discover a power, a strength in the people themselves. The local group possessed the power that comes from information—information about the community, the language, the culture; information about the strengths and weaknesses of people within the community. Those intervening had to discover constructive ways to release the power of the residents. Further, the intervening group had to use its power in a way that the local group could handle and that would allow for the power of both groups to solve the problems at hand.

The use of money, for example, can be overwhelming. The social service agency provided a base to which funds could be given and protected for the community. However, only the community council decided how that money would be used. Training programs taught people how to use the banking system, how to get welfare checks to a safe place,and how to do simple bookkeeping.

"Shared power" became a key concept in this experience. In a real sense, the power of the outside group became incarnate in the local group. The people became truly empowered, strong, able to live. Out of those sessions, people began to wrestle with the meaning of their lives and the values by which they lived.

Through this process, members of this new community found the opportunity for self-expression. The residents of each floor of the apartment building designed the hallways—put up their own signs, directions, decorations. This opportunity allowed for increased self-awareness as individuals and identity as a people. As they found means of expressing the new empowerment, they began to have confidence in this "power to be" as theirs.

The condition of those apartments today, I do not know; but the excitement of being a leader in that intervention and seeing that change, I shall never forget. The price of human dignity is constant vigilance; but those years showed what can happen when attention is given to corporate suffering. For that period of time, it was a success story. The suffering work was allowed to take place. Note the following factors in that success:

1. The process was allowed to develop slowly. Those helping began work a year before the first person moved into the building.

2. As the group formed and there was turnover in the apartments, only the number the group could assimilate was allowed to enter.

3. In that assimilation, time was taken to deal with emotions—anger, problems of trust, fear, hope, expressions of affirmation.

4. Cultural roots received careful attention. The community looked at its past. People learned to let go of the past community, yet retain those memories and practices that fit in the new community. (The gift of surrender applied to the group and to the individuals.)

5. The tenants discovered symbols that reflected the new community—the new group. The signs and decorations on each floor were a type of confession—not of sin, but of faith. As symbols that expressed a positive identity emerged, a type of resurrection happened before our eyes. The group needed to affirm that "resurrection" and new life. The symbols provided that affirmation.

The presence of "outsiders" once threatened the neighborhood. That presence now became a basis for dealing with the suffering. The group began to find meaning, and in that meaning, a sense of purpose developed.

What about the cosmic dimension in this experience? Since many of the people were Roman Catholic, the Mass came to have more and more meaning for them as a sense of community developed. However, it is a mistake to believe that the cosmic dimension is expressed only and always in traditional religious symbols. In the group work and opportunity for discussion, each person began to deal with personal meanings and values, and the group, too, sensed its values. For example, one person began to draw pictures of the others in the group. Her artwork was remarkable for someone untrained. She shared her work with others. When asked the meaning of the picture of a man sitting by a fruit stand in the ghetto, she replied, "I once saw only tragedy in those old men; but the fruit stand is there because now I begin to see the hope of God." The cosmic was there.

This story reflects only one slice of life. Yet it illustrates basic factors in corporate suffering work.

B. The second experience of suffering comes from a study of poverty in India. Whether or not people agree, all can learn from different approaches to suffering. My visit to a village near Nagpur showed me once again that intervention in the area of suffering must take into account both the structure of the individual and that of the community.

Nagpur is a city of a million inhabitants, located in the center of India. The village itself, a few miles outside the city, contains several hundred people who live in mud huts in the most desperate squalor. Unlike their counterparts in the city, at least these poorest of the poor can see the sun. Children roam the surrounding fields in safety. The other side of the difference from their city counterparts, however, concerns the elements. These people have no freedom from the heat of the sun and no place of escape from the power of the monsoon.

An American missionary doctor, Ronald Seaton, drove me to this village. We accompanied an Indian social worker and several nurses in training—some were government nurses and some were from Mure Hospital, a Christian hospital. When we arrived after traveling over the bumpy road—formed more by use than by engineering—women and children emerged from every side. The social worker, a man, immediately went to a particular hut. The woman who greeted him had been chosen by the villagers as their volunteer for the hospital. The nurses and social worker talked with the woman; then, based on the information she gave them, fanned out through the village.

The volunteer had a role: to know the condition and need of every member of the community; to let the nurses know who needed to be seen and who did not, who had illness and who did not; to hear instructions from the nurses and to remind the villagers of those instructions. The volunteer had authority; support from the village chief insured that authority.

As we walked around, we saw that some of the children were totally naked. Few men were to be seen. The lucky ones were away at jobs and earning four rupees a day (about forty cents).

I shall never forget the face of a woman who looked to be fifty. (She was closer to twenty). As I stood in the sun with my expensive camera and lightweight summer clothes—their price would have equaled a half year's wages locally—the woman walked by. When she was some ten feet to my left, we looked at each other. Our eyes caught. She moved quickly; and in her step and face, I saw nothing but anger.

I mentioned this anger later to the social worker and said that I could well understand the feelings she must have had.

"No," said the social worker, "I think you have projected." He went on, "In her situation, you would be angry. You have the ego strength with which to be angry. I wish she had anger; that would be a sign of hope. What you saw in her face was no emotion at all. She has learned to cope with her situation by cutting off feeling. She probably just observed that you were there and dealt with you as though you were not. That is her defense for survival."

By the time the nurses left to call on the people they had to see, I had attracted a small crowd of children. They stared with fascination at my skin, my camera, me. Since we were standing near a post, a game developed. One shy boy looked at me from behind the post. I mimicked a hide-and-seek game with him. The act brought giggles, a smile. Then another face emerged; another gesture of mimic. Suddenly, genuine laughter from all sides enveloped me. We played the game for several minutes.

I then motioned with my camera. Indian children—indeed, all children—love to have their picture taken. I took several at different shutter openings and speeds. My actions said to these children, "You are of worth—important enough for this kind of attention and care."

When it was time to leave, we waved good-bye. As we drove away, the momentary sense of warmth from the relationship with the children was invaded by the reality of the poverty as I noticed human feces along the road. Those same children and their parents would step aside and relieve themselves as nature urged. Other children would then play in the same area. The rains washed the excrement away—sometimes back into the village itself.

What do we see in this area of corporate intervention?

Dorothee Sölle identifies three phases, or stages, in the battle of suffering.[1] Phase one is the mute stage—numbness, explosiveness, speechlessness, isolation. Phase two is the lamenting stage. Here, one takes on and sometimes even wins the battle within given structures. Phase three brings us to solidarity with others. Powerlessness becomes empowerment.

Dr. Sölle's stages help us gain a sense of the suffering process. Yet we still have much to learn. Sociologists at the Christian Institute in Nagpur told me that they are questioning the traditional and Western studies of poverty. They feel that out of the Indian culture itself come catagories different from ours, which need consideration.

Their new research may well help us with our understanding of corporate suffering. Dr. Sölle's three categories may carry the same danger as all efforts to divide human experience into types—that is, we may take them too seriously. One individual, for example, will move in and out of phases one and two or phases two and three. The different phases may be experienced in the same day. The phases may, in fact, reflect different groups and different times in the same day. No one fits the types exactly.

Nevertheless, awareness of phases does suggest something about the care of the suffering group. We cannot look at the Nagpur village as though there were not differences in the phases of the various individuals. The woman who attracted my attention demonstrated the mute or numb phase. The children, as a group and as individuals, gave a mixture of examples. Some showed the lamenting phase in which people cope with the moment but make no changes in their situation. The volunteer leader of the community reflected the changing phase. She could make changes and work toward change.

In seeking to bring care to this group, the Mure Hospital had shifted its approach to medical care in two ways. The traditional approach had been that of one to one, and of dealing with specific diseases. The emphasis centered on curing. Now the emphasis centers on "wellness." This means an emphasis on preventive medicine, a need to look at the cluster of relationships that allow for wellness, and an approach not just to the individual but to the group. This shift from illness to wellness and from the individual to the group has proven workable and effective.

Today the medical care givers of that hospital look at the structure of the society as much as at the structure of the individual. The care giver now asks, "What leads to wellness of all?"—not just "How do I heal this one?" Not far from the village, the hospital leadership established a center that included a clinic, but also included homes. Nagpur itself housed the hospital. The three-pronged approach included:

1. Insistence that if an individual had to leave the village for the hospital, the entire family became

involved: The family went to the hospital or the clinic. Healing became a family matter. The illness became an opportunity to reach the wider group and affect the system, not merely the individual. The cluster, as it were, received attention.

2. Creation of a model village in which mothers could bring their children for innoculation: Children received treatment; mothers learned how to produce as well as to prepare food. Mushrooms have great nutrient value. By seeding little six-by-twelve-inch bales of straw, mushrooms could bring income to the family as well as nutrition of high value.

In this way, the hospital changed the structure of the economy and the use of the land. The housing in the small area brought actual improvement to some families and set a model for others. The social worker lived in this model village and became the center for learning new ways of living, community decision making, and situational change.

3. Discovery of a new way of sanitation: Outhouses were ineffective because no one used them. However, pigs proved to be excellent scavengers of human refuse. By sending out pigs daily along the paths where people left their droppings, the trails and roads could be cleaned. That may seem primitive to those of us accustomed to great modern sanitation plants, but the plan worked. The conditions for wellness improved.

By going into the village on a regular basis, power truly came into a center of powerlessness. The presence of the nurses and the social worker symbolized an avenue of change. Even the mute women saw this outer power come into their midst. Some of the women who had moved into Dr. Sölle's lamenting phase had once been in the mute phase. As the presence of those with power increased, trust developed, and some moved ultimately to the conviction that they did have power to improve their situation.

These interventions, then, were at the physical, social, and cosmic levels. The approach to the physical levels addressed not only physical illnesses but also the physical problems of housing, sanitation, and farming. The hospital looked seriously at the cluster. At the social level, the community relationship and process of community building altered structures. Even my short time of play with the youngsters became part of that community building. My pictures were of the group together. They laughed at me—together.

The cosmic dimension must not be overlooked. The act of bringing an outer power into the midst of the situation communicated to the villagers a power greater than themselves—a power now available to them. The power was not God as we think of God, but the process began an awareness of power beyond the local horizon. That awareness should not be overlooked. Ability to sense a greater power, even if only human, can be a first step to sensing God's power.

In the small group sessions, the social worker built on that awareness. One of the needs he addressed related to the cosmic dimension on a religious level. At issue in India is the feeling, "I can do nothing; my situation is my karma." By contrast, the Christian witness that change is possible, that change can come before death and reincarnation, formed the motivation for making a difference. The social worker had, and still has, the task of helping the people in the village understand the cosmic dimension in their lives. He needed to help them gain a meaning—a faith—that made sense of the realities they faced.

Because of this fact, the Christian church has often been the change agent in many parts of India. In Madras, during a drought, the church led in digging wells. The government later followed that lead. In Nagpur, the church under Bishop Bhandare led a strike which caused a change in the law so that rickshaw drivers could own their rigs—permitting them to earn a wage above the poverty level. The Christian awareness of the cosmic allowed for that suffering work, which moved a people from an impossible past to a promising future.

Part of the task of the social worker in discussions at Nagpur focused on helping people find symbols that allowed them to make sense out of the changes that could come in their lives. The dimension of finding those symbols and expressing them is as much a part of the care-giving task as is the healing of the wounds themselves. More will be said about symbols in Chapter 6.

C. The preceding instances of intervention in suffering dealt with corporate pain which reflected the different stages of suffering in different individuals. There come times when a tragedy or disaster is not chronic but acute. (Chronic suffering is long-term. Acute suffering is sudden.) When the suffering is acute, all members of the group are suddenly reduced to the same level. The assassination of John F. Kennedy proved just such an acute time.

The dynamics of change within a galvanizing tragedy has its beneficial moments. A national tragedy may bring a people together. A child killed in a neighborhood brings the people together in a new way. Sometimes we take the risk of that suffering. At a college ball game, for example, defeat brings its suffering as a student body seeks to deal with the loss. The sending of astronauts into space runs the risk of acute tragedy. Lose one of those flights, and the nation and beyond will feel the effect. Whether we choose the risk or not, the suffering hurts.

The means of dealing with public suffering may be through radio or television, at a school or business assembly, at a public rally, or at church. Aristotle identified one of the oldest means of intervention in his *Poetics*: catharsis. Aristotle took his cue from the experience of Greek tragedy. In effect, he asked why people went time and again to see a tragedy they had seen before. One difference between a tragedy and a mystery is that the people may know the outcome of a tragedy in advance, but will still see repeat performances. Once a person has seen a mystery, unless for nostalgia's sake or to see good acting, a viewer will not return. The Greek tragedy, however, people attended again and again.

Aristotle found the answer for this interest in the experience of catharsis. A cathartic cleanses. By living through the tragedy, Aristotle observed, the members of the audience found a catharsis, a cleansing, that freed the soul. Reliving the experience allowed people to go out of the theater renewed and ready for the problems of the day.

Catharsis may help move a group from the phase of numbness to the phase of action. In the experience of today, too little attention is paid to this tool of social intervention. This tool, in addition to others, might well be used.

The actions of the American public at the time of John Kennedy's death show how catharsis helps in the process of group suffering. When the announcement came, "President Kennedy has been shot," all changed. A parishioner and I no longer focused on the family member of whom we were speaking, but on the radio. Soon at homes across the land, people gathered around radios and television sets. Television informed us of new events, but also showed us past events. The repetition provided catharsis. All knew the story. Yet, seeing it again and again became a means of trying to absorb it, deal with it. Some of the President's speeches and statements were repeated. A whole people had become part of John F. Kennedy's life, and through television, he had become part of theirs.

Another problem developed: guilt. In the days before his death, derisive statements had centered on John Kennedy and his family as he moved toward the vulnerability and exposure of an election year. A comedian's record mimicking the presidential family sold wildly. As I recall it, the recording was quite good, yet parts of it were close to improper. In one such part, a supposed conversation between Kennedy and Lincoln, Mr. Lincoln suggested a cure for Mr. Kennedy's problems. Lincoln suggested, "Try the theater," a reference to his experience at the Ford Theater. Because of such material, guilt gripped the nation. That corporate numbness needed the healing process of suffering.

How should ministers have handled that day? Many had sermons already prepared—it was Thanksgiving Sunday. Red, the color for both martyrs and country, was displayed in some churches. That itself had an immediate symbolic effect: "This Sunday is different." It said that the congregation was part of a suffering community—a community larger than itself. The color said that the congregation's suffering dwarfed even the sense of the suffering of the Pilgrims.

Some clergy chose to make no change in their plans. They thus exhibited either massive denial of what had taken place or simply lack of confidence. Most made adjustments. In some instances, the call to worship, the hymns, the prayers all sought to bring to consciousness the meaning of the day and the symbols.

How would the sermon be presented?

My own experience proved both ironic and meaningful. The planned sermon began, "If this were a day of national tragedy, could we still give thanks?" The background of the sermon was the second chapter of Mark, which tells of the paralytic whose sins Jesus forgave and who then took up his bed and walked. The sermon sought to acknowledge the forgiveness of God, lift to awareness that that forgiveness allows us the freedom to look at personal sins and failures, and brings a sense of God's care.

In the look at oneself, the sermon spoke to the feelings of guilt. I observed that no one of us had pulled the trigger and that all of us abhorred the act. Yet the sermon went on to point out that there had been ways in which people actually, or in thought, had dehumanized the President: anti-Catholic statements, jokes at the expense of the White House family, secret thoughts of "I wish he were dead."

As I look back on the event, the point I remember most is that lifting up where many people had been, identifying the corporate nature of our experience, and affirming the reality of God's love, did something. Part of the discussion brought a catharsis both for me and for the congregation. Part of the worship allowed us to bring to our conscious minds what we needed and to find those symbols that dealt with both the pain and the freedom to move beyond the pain.

Although at that time the pastoral prayer was not given after the sermon, on that occasion I gave a fuller post-sermon prayer than usual. It read in part:

> O Lord, much, we find, is not in our hands. Yet, so much as is, we bring to you. Grant that, aware of our own weaknesses and need to be forgiven, we may move out to be strong citizens of this land, to uphold the value of life, and to discover anew what it means to be a nation under God. As our grief has made us one, as we have sensed the oneness of your forgiving presence, lead us forward now to pick up the unfinished tasks of this nation and of our personal lives. Thus, may not evil but your goodwill be affirmed, and may we be brought the nearer to your Kingdom; through Jesus Christ our Lord. Amen.

Unlike the other two experiences mentioned—the apartment building in the city and the village in India—cultural divergence did not figure prominently here. Emotional, not physical pain was the issue. Pastors could therefore focus on the group sense of pain and loss. We could concentrate on the flow from guilt to forgiveness, from bondage to freedom.

In these three cases, suffering work involved attention to both structure and process, both the group and the individual. Structures had to change if the specific needs were to be met and the process allowed—the process that would open the way for healing and could prevent further evil. In these cases, the matter of spiritual intervention did not mean ignoring the material and intellectual aspects of the problems, but seeing that the spiritual was expressed through them. The woman in the Bronx, for example, saw the cosmic in the man on the street. The social worker in India had to deal with the cosmic in order to provide for new opportunity. All that helped the helper facilitate the suffering work. (The role of the service of divine worship in the therapeutic process has been developed in lectures, courses, and books by numerous authors, including this one.[2])

In brief summary, then, what tools of intervention relate to group suffering? We have spoken of:

1. awareness of the cluster;
2. an approach that deals with all aspects of the cluster, not just the individual;
3. attention to the structures and the changes that must be made to help the group or the individual;
4. catharsis;
5. time for the process to take place;
6. surrender;
7. the discovery and use of symbols that allow for dealing with public and personal guilt, public and personal forgiveness.

Individual Suffering

We turn now from the suffering group to the suffering person. Aware that we as individuals are always in relation to some group, the fact is that suffering work goes on in each of us privately just as it goes on in a group corporately. Groups suffer. Persons suffer.[3]

A. The first "case" I have chosen comes from my personal struggle. Those trained in counseling may question its use. After all, counselors do not impose their problems on clients—why impose one's own story on the reader? Yet none of us comes to the healing process without a background of experience. That background, in fact, becomes part of the process. Therefore I present this personal situation because it helped open my eyes to some aspects of the dynamic of suffering. As such, this case not only speaks to the issue of this chapter—suffering work—but shows how that suffering work can take place in a person who ministers to suffering in others.

Further, as we will discuss more in depth when we talk about the healer, the healer also suffers. If a healer does not experience suffering work, there will be no capacity to heal. Therefore, this instance becomes a basis not only for judging my own perspective, but also for sensing more data on suffering work and for beginning to express thoughts about the healer in suffering.

The experience centers around the death of my mother. I was in my early fifties. My mother had a long-time problem with her circulatory system, but good medical guidance and a disciplined life had allowed her more than seventy productive years. In her seventy-eighth year, however, she began to fail and in her seventy-ninth, she died.

Those last years proved to be quality time. Points of reconciliation were experienced where they had been needed. I could minister to her during the last year; and her death became a time of deep meaning, emotion, and wholeness. I felt that my grief was good. With my background and experience, I "of course" knew exactly how to handle the break.

Life should be so sure and so simple! The gift of surrender does not come easily.

In the two months that followed her death, I found myself unable to relate to others in grief. This was especially true at times of funerals. Oh, all the right words were said—and said with effect . . . but I was not in it. Something was wrong.

In working with the terminally ill, I had the opportunity to serve with a team of oncologists, radiologists, and psychologists. I sought out one of the psychologists. The following is an excerpt from the sixty minutes I spent with him:

Minister 1: I have always thought of myself as a feeling person, but now I have none. No feelings at all when I conduct a funeral.

Psychologist 1: For you, that is unusual.

M2: I have really come with a specific request. I do not want to be hypnotized. But I would appreciate your leading me through the imaging exercises in order to deal with this.

(After some discussion, the psychologist agreed and the process began.)

P2: You know how to relax. Just take a few minutes and let me know when you are ready.

M3: (after a few moments of relaxation exercises) I am ready.

P3: I would like you to imagine a spot you like of quiet and beauty. Tell me about it.

M4: It is a spot in the mountains. Granite rocks move up from the side of a beautiful mountain lake. The lake has a green color—like a glacial lake. Grass and moss go down to the lake. On the far side, I see a snowbank. The sky is blue—a deep blue.

P4: Imagine a cave. It is a tunnel that goes deep into the mountain and comes out the other side. Imagine yourself going into the tunnel and coming out. What do you see?

M5: I see a great expanse. Like the fields of Kansas grain or corn. It is like Katherine Bates' song, "for amber waves . . . ."

P5: As you look, is anyone with you, or are you alone?

M6: Alone, very alone.

P6: Place yourself, now, on a magic carpet. Imagine yourself flying across the fields. As you go, you see signs that go back year by year. This year. Last year. Go by them as far back as you can remember. Now, what year is it?

M7: It is 1930. I am four.

P7: What is happening? What do you remember?

M8: My earliest memory is of my father leaving the house to go to the hospital.

P8: Can you tell me about it?

(The scene is described in considerable detail—the clothes I wore, the kind of day.)

P9: What happens?

P10: My father says, "I must leave you now. Take care of your mother."

(Quiet tears begin to form and run down my cheeks.)

P10: Anything else? Do you cry?

M11: No crying. Nothing else.

P11: Tell me the next memory as you come forward.

(There are then told a series of stories—all of them having to do with separation—as the years are recalled.)

M12: I suddenly have a thought.

P12: What is that?

M13: Christ said, "I will not leave you comfortless." It is as though everything can be very close. Christ is very real. God is very near.

P13: That can happen with significant religious figures.

M14: Yes. This is important for me. It is as though he had known all the

> separations in life. He understands the feeling. And when you know someone is with you in the feeling of separation, you are not as separate anymore.

The session ended with a description again of my mother's death, of the funeral, and of the burial. Tears flowed easily and quietly. I felt very much at peace after a hard morning.

The key in this experience of suffering work was the discovery that any point of suffering touches all the other points of suffering in a person's experience. The therapist had taken me back to each point of separation and allowed me to reintegrate that point again in the light of this fundamental separation—the break from my mother. The gift of surrender of my mother came only after reaffirming the surrender of many past experiences.

More research is needed to decide whether any experience of suffering opens up the past. Probably many points of suffering can be handled by a thought, by a repression, by putting it out of our minds as we go about our daily business. Yet there come moments when the pain and the suffering are deep enough that the standard defenses will not suffice.

Without defenses against pain, we could not function. There is nothing wrong with having defenses. The "wrong" comes in those moments when the suffering is so great that the usual defenses break down and we do not deal with the break. The death of a mother—the person who gave birth to one and nurtured one—is such a moment. Necessity then demands going back and reintegrating the past experiences of suffering so that the new suffering moments become part of one. For that to happen, the symbols that once allowed for the healing and reflected the healing must take on a new meaning. To be effective, the symbols need to be recharged, as it were. Note how that happened here.

Christ means much to me. My own view of Christ is different from that of the therapist. The response of the therapist, professional in every way, allowed me to work out my meaning of Christ in this new experience. From that time on, the sacrament of Communion, the experience of prayer, the study of the Bible, would have new impact for me.

Suffering work not only deals with pain—it allows for the new expression of healing that in fact makes the healing alive. In my own way, my statement, "Everything can be very close. Christ is very real. God is very near," became my new confession of faith. Christ became the means of expressing that whole process of separation and closeness.

This experience suggests the importance in worship and in counseling of allowing for a relation between symbol and process. In the nurturing experience, we can look at the facts of history, the events of the day, the stories of Scripture, the facts of science, and allow them to become part of us. In the worship experience, we seek again and again the symbols that express the new relationship. The task of the liturgist is to help find those liturgical symbols which bring that relationship alive.

The approach of the psychologist would not have been appropriate at all times. The approach he used allowed me to withdraw into myself. Such withdrawal could be escape; it could be misused and allow for manipulation; it might have been something I could not handle—especially if I had been on drugs, or had trouble knowing the difference between fantasy and reality. Mass use of the imaging technique can be damaging because it can allow for a sense of euphoria and well-being without an awareness of the difference between induced relaxation and the true wrestling that is suffering work.

In this instance, however, the approach was appropriate. I had good inner strength and a good sense of identity. I needed only an opportunity to relate a traumatic moment in my life to that identity. The suffering work allowed that opportunity.

My experience also demonstrates that suffering work is not only for those in a moment of deep tragedy. Here, as with the congregation that faced the death of John F. Kennedy, we have an instance of suffering in the midst of general health.

B. I wish to share a second instance, which I call suffering unto life. Søren Kierkegaard spoke of "suffering unto death." Kierkegaard had a profound sense of the power of suffering work. Both his *Either/Or* and his *Sickness unto Death* are reflections on suffering work.

Yet, as is often the case with people who deal with the need to be rid of the idols in our lives—the sham part of life—Kierkegaard did not give much attention to the power and healing side. At least for me, his confessions of sin were stronger than his confessions of faith.

Kierkegaard, through his writings, proved helpful to me personally. The honesty of his wrestling with depression, his concern for the sterile approach of the church and the liturgy, and his discovery of the healing that did come in his moments of spiritual breakthrough touched me at various times in my own struggle with faith.

Kierkegaard's *Purity of Heart* comes close to what is still important for me in the experience of suffering work. Yet, even there, his emphasis on that moment of silence in worship before God, when we are confronted by the Almighty and see ourselves "as we really are," quickly becomes interpreted as "how bad we really are." The completion of Kierkegaard's process must also include seeing what, through the suffering work, we have become. The confession of faith is as critical as the confession of sin. In fact, failure to confess the healing and the strengths becomes the new sin, for it is failure to accept, in its fullness, what God has created. (Here again, the gift of surrender must include surrender to victory.)

This second case study involves a hospital call. Bill was a parishioner who had not yet found healing of a terrible back problem. Yet there were moments of periodic healing and wholeness in the process toward the ultimate goal. As suggested in Chapter 3, our concern for healing must recognize that healing itself follows developmental processes. As one deals with suffering, the emotions may move back through life so that any of us feel and act at an infantile level. As we begin to recover, we move forward and touch the various levels. As we progress—learn to crawl, as it were, and then walk and then run—the different stages of accomplishment are themselves levels of healing. These levels must be acknowledged so that they become truly part of us.

A person who has been cured of lameness and does not get up to walk, for example, has not experienced full healing. The physical reality has not become a personal reality. Mark 2:11, in which Jesus commands, "Rise," recognized the necessity of "owning" the healing.

The surgeon said that Bill had one of the most badly damaged backs he had ever seen. Spurs and crushed discs pressed on the spine. Four operations were necessary before all infection was cleared and healing could begin. Bill's tolerance to pain killers became such that he could not take enough to dull the pain. His pain was as great as any I had ever seen.

One morning when I went to his hospital room, Bill was struggling to come out of the bathroom. I saw his fingers inch around the door, much like the strange fingers of E.T. in the movie. As Bill slowly moved out, the agony on his face led to a contortion that might amaze even E.T.

Bill had slipped to a point of total dependence on others—as dependent as a newborn infant. On this occasion, he sought to move out of that state and take his first steps. It would have been easy to stay at the first level of infancy. Instead, he undertook the task of moving from that stage to the next.

As we talked, he spoke of the long nights, the need to sleep, the impossibility of sleep, the irrelevance of television ("Even 'I Love Lucy' doesn't help," he said.).

Relaxation techniques are being used more and more to help control pain. I asked Bill about it. He replied that it helped some but that it was hard to do alone. He asked for help with the process. I took him through the routine of tensing muscles and then relaxing them (of course avoiding the muscles in the area of the surgery). With his eyes closed, Bill imagined a spot he liked (it was his living room with the Christmas tree), and then imagined Christ as being with him there in that spot. I then offered the following prayer:

Lord, you know Bill better than I do. You know his pain and the feeling of having been left alone. You know even the feeling that God does not care. Lord, place your hand on Bill's head even as I do. Grant unto him the ability to allow the inner healing powers to be at work. Allow the infection to respond to the treatment and the convalescence to begin. Whatever pain there is to be, grant Bill that sense of your presence which will allow him to endure. We hear you say, as you said in Scripture, "To him who endures, I will give the tree of life."

With that, I pronouced the familiar benediction, "May the Lord bless you and keep you . . . ."

After a time of quiet with no comment, Bill said the pain had receded. "Somehow, now I feel on top of it," he said. He talked about his visualization—his living room—and then began to speak of his time working in a kibbutz in Israel. Combining the sense of the Holy Land with the sense of his home, he said, made the prayer meaningful to him. The conversation continued around home, favorite memories. The optimistic note proved a sharp contrast to the pessimistic beginning. Bill had moved from the pain to an awareness of the strength that was there. The discussion of the Holy Land and his living room became a means of affirming those symbols that reflected the strength in his life.

People often feel they must use a particular religious language or medical jargon in order to give evidence of true healing. With Bill, talk of the Holy Land and his careful restating of what had come alive to him there served as his praise to God "from whom all blessings flow." He did not need to use the actual words to make the point.

The conversation which allowed for symbolization of those things that were of strength and peace was as important as the expression of the pain and all the problems. We therefore see that suffering work moves to a future orientation; it does not stay with the past. Whereas Kierkegaard wrote of *Sickness unto Death,* here we have suffering unto life.

Aware that this move to a new level is just a stage on the road to full health, it is important that the new expression of faith not become the new legalism. The expression of faith is just that—an expression. It becomes the foundation from which to move to the next level; it is not the next level. Paul expressed the mood when he wrote, "Not as though I had already attained . . . but this one thing I do . . . I press toward the mark . . . the high calling of God in Christ Jesus" (Phil. 3:12, 13, 14).

C. The final instance I wish to share is a composite based on reports from several students and colleagues in San Francisco and Berkeley, California. As the first example centered on suffering in one who usually is the healer, and the second centered on suffering in one in great pain, this instance shows how suffering work affects both the care giver and the care receiver.

This particular experience also shows the individual dimension of corporate suffering, which must accompany the corporate dimension of individual suffering. For those who bring care, this knowledge is critical. It requires us to recognize that there are times when the patient serves as healer and the healer needs the help of the patient. This awareness forbids our becoming manipulative and arrogant as care givers. Rather, it requires a humility that sees both the care giver and the care receiver as part of a process in which both suffer and both receive healing.

On this particular occasion Fred, a pastor, called on a member of his community who had AIDS (Acquired Immunity Deficiency Syndrome). The discovery of AIDS has caused many emotions—fear, anger, questioning, guilt. It also has led to increased understanding on the part of both "straight" and "gay" people who have sought to minister to the situation. There are religious and political issues surrounding the condition, but that is not our interest here. We will look at the dialogue to see an instance of suffering work that affected Fred as well as his client, Joseph.

The first time he visited Joseph in the hospital, Fred was struck with fear. He had read about AIDS. Now he was seeing a friend who might be dead within a month. The disease suddenly had become a part of Fred's life—even though he did not have it. Not knowing what to expect, he went to the hospital.

Joseph proved to be a remarkable individual. He had studied AIDS thoroughly and told Fred more about it than Fred knew enough to ask. Joseph expressed his own feelings about the danger of death and then asked, "Fred, what are your own fears?"

In reflecting on the experience, Fred suddenly discovered a new healing. Joseph had given him so much information that he no longer wondered what Kaposi's sarcoma lesions looked like—Joseph had shown them. He did not need to wonder about face masks, or about death, or about the unknown. As Fred wrote in his diary, "I no longer had to fear 'the unknown' because I had seen the 'beast,' and, to the extent that was possible, the 'beast had been named' in that first visit."

Here again we see the process of suffering work as it helps the sufferer find a symbol for coming to terms with the pain. Fred suffered; Joseph suffered. As Joseph suffered, he sought to find names to identify the pain and the problem. When Fred came on the scene, Joseph shared those names with Fred and allowed Fred to make them his own. The suffering work for both men meant facing the reality of AIDS in such a way that the facts could be transformed from something "out there" into an integrated part of each individual. The process of symbolizing allowed that integration to take place.

A model for that process appears in the book of Genesis; when Adam named the beasts of the field, the very naming was part of the process for gaining power over them. We must remember that a name, in ancient Hebrew, described the individual—it gave the identity. Bethlehem means *house of God;* Joshua means *savior*. Even today, if someone came up to a man and called him by name, the man might reply, "You have the advantage over me." By not knowing the visitor's name when the visitor knew something of the nature of the man—at least his name—the visitor had power, an advantage. Hence, Adam's naming of the beasts allowed him to have power over them. With that power, he could exercise his stewardship.

In the suffering work of this interview, Fred, as the helper, needed those names, those symbols, which could give him power over the beast called AIDS. That very work allowed Fred to find healing and move on in his relations with Joseph and others.

In a later interview, Fred realized that he had not touched Joseph. There had been no handshake. There had been only an antiseptic distance. The disease is not transmitted through touch, but anxiety had resulted in the defense of distance. On his next visit, Fred gave Joseph a hug. He had thought about Jesus and the lepers and had become conscious of what a touch communicated. For Fred, the touch communicated an affirmation of his own healing. The touch may have been more important for Fred, as the care giver, than for Joseph. Fred needed to give the hug as a symbol of his own victory in the suffering work. In the context of that healing, Joseph himself could then move from Fred's suffering to his own.

I

Now, in looking back at suffering work, there emerge guidelines for the care giver. The key model is that of servanthood. The care giver is not a servant to the person who is suffering, however, but to the process of healing which touches them both. In Christian terms, this is surrender to the Holy Spirit. This sense of servanthood rejects all techniques used just for the sake of techniques. Some insist on quoting passages of Scripture as though they were texts that promise results. Others avoid Scripture and prayer as though using either would be too pious or even magical. This sense of servanthood rejects both approaches as techniques and seeks to allow for the process of health itself.

The task of the care giver in the servanthood model requires helping others to find that which allows suffering work to take place. Part of that process involves finding symbols that will make the healing real.

From this model of servanthood, we can identify five guidelines for care in the suffering moment:

1. Empathy. Empathy is the capacity to feel where the other is and to let that feeling become part of "you" as care giver. It is the capacity to suffer with the sufferer, but not to lose one's identity in the sufferer. Empathy is a dynamic that became familiar in the counseling process during the 1950s.

2. Naming. Naming is finding those symbols that come alive and make real the nature of the suffering, the experience of the suffering work, and the nature of the healing. This process allows us to integrate the experiences of both sickness and health in a way that allows for a full life. It allows us to be on top of what

breaks in on us and not be cast down by it. The process takes seriously the gift of surrender.

3. Relating. Relating is coming to terms with oneself in the suffering moment, with those who are significant in the community of a suffering moment, and with the cosmos.

4. Consciousness-raising. Consciousness-raising became a critical experience for women in the liberation movement. Actually, consciousness-raising is necessary for all liberation. Another word for this might be *sensitizing*. It is the work of lifting up, into an area where we can see and handle them, the various parts of the painful time which allows for the suffering work.

This consciousness-raising must take place at the three levels of awareness—self, community, cosmos. It must deal with one's roots, the cluster of circumstances that relate to the pain and the symbol work (described in Chapter 6).

5. Prayer-Scripture-Meditation. These tools allow for relation to whatever transcends us, so that we ourselves may transcend the situation which causes the suffering. Through the experience, we may sense that we are part of that which is cosmic, that we wrestle against more than just flesh and blood.

The goal in suffering work is so to confront evil and be freed from delusional spirituality that we achieve true maturity and wholeness. In biblical terms, suffering work defines what happens when one says "I am in Christ," or "Christ is in me." To be "in Christ" means being in that context which endures the pain of separation, of care for others, of servanthood, and of finding means to express all of that. Suffering work also defines what it means to possess that which "names the beast," which causes surrender, which brings power over problems, and which, biblically, Paul calls "Christ in you."

In looking back at suffering work, we have spoken as though suffering were always a matter of extremes. The Holocaust was an extreme experience. Bill, with his back surgery, endured extreme pain. Joseph, facing death, was in an extreme situation. But we must remember that suffering comes in mild forms as many times as it comes in extreme forms. A person puts in a hard day of work, returns home, and says, "I'm tired." A young person begins to raise questions about identity—not deep soul-searching questions, but the daily "Where do I fit in?" type of question. Suffering work shows itself in these forms as often as in the extremes.

Suffering work is as much a factor in the so-called mild moments as in the crisis moments. At these points, the experience of prayer and meditation have much to offer. The daily experience of meditation is a discipline which, when truly followed, allows one to be prepared for the big crises when they come. In such moments, the task of being in touch with the reality of the forces at work in one's life is paramount. All who suffer must allow for letting go what is demonic and taking hold of what is healing.

Consider Psalm 51. This psalm may be used at almost any level of suffering. The task in using it, as in any moment of devotion, is not to worry about what one does not understand, but concentrate on what one does understand. How does the psalm put us in touch with the cosmic, with others, with ourselves? Those are questions to ask while reading and thinking about the psalm.

For example, a phrase in the psalm says, "In sin did my mother conceive me"(vs. 5). Does this mean that sex is evil? Or is the text simply unclear? In either case, in devotional use of the psalm, do not worry about what seems unclear, but stay with what is clear. As we go on, perhaps there comes a moment when the words leap out: "The sacrifices of God are a broken spirit: a broken and a contrite heart, O God, thou wilt not despise" (vs. 17). Now, there is a passage that touches me. I am tired and weighed down. All I can offer is my tiredness . . . but God accepts that tiredness. Awareness of that acceptance puts me in touch with the cosmic, allows me to accept myself, and frees me in relation to everyone else.

On another occasion, having become more aware of the solidarity of human life and the pervasive nature of evil in the world, we may read the passage again. As we comes to the part that says "In sin did my mother conceive me," a new meaning emerges. The passage may speak in a new way. We may understand that there is nothing in the world that does not have in it a dimension of evil. We need to "name that beast" if we are to deal with it. The psalm speaks in a different, deeper way than before—it names the beast. The psalm expresses the reality of evil. The psalm expresses the reality of forgiveness.

Suffering work requires time to allow a person, a piece of writing, a passage of Scripture, to speak so that the sufferer does not make a god out of the suffering itself.

From this discussion of suffering work as a process, we now move to a new aspect of the question "How do I, as a care giver, help?" In the new aspect, the issue is not just one of my techniques, but of me. Who am I as healer? We turn, then, to the chapter titled "The Suffering Healer—The Healed Healer."

CHAPTER V

The Suffering Healer—The Healed Healer

The key message of this chapter can be expressed in one sentence: Out of the suffering healer comes the healed healer, and only the healed healer truly heals. There we have a paradox in its true sense. The word *paradox,* from the Greek, means two parallel—though seemingly contradictory—teachings that must be taken together.[1] This paradox is not actually contradictory, but contains two dimensions of a total truth: Only the healed person truly heals, and only the person who knows suffering is truly healed.

This fact has a practical consequence for the person who would heal. There must be time to deal with the personal suffering. Healing takes something out of each of us; much energy is expended. Modern discussion of "burn out" among pastors, social workers, doctors, counselors, relates here. After a period of healing, even Jesus had to take a retreat for renewal. Without attention to the energy that suffering-healing takes from us, none of us will last long.

Two insights form the basis for understanding the nature of suffering-healing or the "suffering healer." One understanding relates to the shadow side of life in each of us—including those of us who would bring care and counsel to others. The other understanding relates to the dynamic of this shadow in the healing process itself.

I

The concept of the "shadow" as part of the healing process has become more and more important in the thinking of many of us. Carl Jung brought this concept to the fore[2]; but all of us, Jungian or not, can appreciate its value. In the area of the physics of light, for example, the use of black light has contributed to art and the theater. Alexander's "black belt"—which will be discussed below—comes not from psychology or Jung, but from the physics of light.

For those of us who seek to help, the concept of the shadow has much to offer. However, I must confess to some pause. Although the writings of Jung have helped me most in my initial thinking about the shadow, I disagree somewhat with his concept. Perhaps it is better to say that I see the shadow in a somewhat different light—if I may mix that metaphor.

I understand the shadow not as independent of light, not as the opposite of light or the obstruction of light, but as a dimension of light itself. Jung took much of his view of the shadow from mythology and the study of dreams. His work is creative and helpful. Yet, if one looks at other areas in which the shadow is also important—such as optics or the physics of light—there emerges even more than Jung gave us.

Why make a point of the shadow?

Any of us who grew up in the days of radio remember the drama called "The Shadow." In fact, we probably are better conditioned for this chapter than are some who did not experience those "good old days." The program opened with the announcer saying, "Who knows what evil lurks in the hearts of men?" With imagination stirred and interest quickened, we all answered with the announcer, "The Shadow knows!"

Therein we have a key insight on the matter of the shadow. The shadow side of each of us, largely in the unconscious, can tell us things about ourselves. It will reflect drives, thoughts, ideas we did not know we had. The shadow side of us will sometimes act itself out in strange, tragic, or bizarre ways.

People often use the Jekyll and Hyde story as an example of a split personality. Dr. Jekyll, as the fine, creative, healing doctor-scientist who sought to do good, and Mr. Hyde, as the evil, murdering plunderer, represent the two sides of this split. Both were the same person—or at least were in the same body. From a Jungian point of view, most of us seek to be and live the Jekyll side of life, but all of us also have a Hyde side, a side that may be so repressed we see it only in the shadow part of our dreams.

This concept expands to observations that often seem as far-fetched as they are far-reaching. Nevertheless, increasing evidence requires that we look seriously at the shadow.

One discovery has to do with acting out behavior. (*Acting out* means that a person not only has a destructive thought but finds the compulsion to act it out in abuse, or even in murder.) The shadow side of us may be acted out not just by ourselves but also by others who are closely identified with us. Somerset Maugham tells the story of a pastor who seeks to "save the soul" of a prostitute.[3] He has a great influence on her, and she follows the path of conversion. Then she is suddenly back in the prostitute role. She kills the pastor. Why? The pastor had sought to seduce her.

Everyone could see the fine moral, upright side of the pastor, but his shadow side compelled him to do exactly the opposite. Failure to recognize that dimension of the shadow within himself resulted in his inability to handle it. More than that, it resulted in his inability to help in any real healing. As we will see later, the process of healing the prostitute meant that the pastor also had to heal the prostitute in himself. Knowledge of the shadow and its dynamic is not only helpful for those who would be healers—it is fundamental.

A further development in understanding the shadow side of life relates to acting out—not just in individuals but also in groups. In speaking of group suffering, we mentioned the group personality. A group—a nation or culture or people—may have a shadow side, just as individuals do. We saw this phenomenon earlier in the Exodus experience when the Jews had to deal with the "Pharaoh" in themselves. This same phenomenon appears in other ways.

In a family, an offspring may act out the shadow side of a parent or sibling. Often it is said, "How can two such different children come from the same parents?" The "nice boy" sees the shadow side acted out in the "bad kid" brother, or the "bad girl" may be acted out in the sister. The wild so-called preacher's kid, or the educator's offspring who simply will not be educated may be reflections of the shadow side in a family.

In the nation, "peace-loving" Americans' fascination with horror movies, violence, and bad news may reflect our shadow side. I still puzzle at the antiabortionist who champions (I do not mean merely assents to, but actually *promotes)* capital punishment; and many who oppose capital punishment give not a second thought to abortion. I have not seen studies to demonstrate this, but perhaps here we see the shadow side of different faiths, religious groups, cultures.

All this seems to suggest that the shadow side of us is always evil. The old radio program even suggested that the shadow is something more profound than just an example of evil. The Shadow, after all, was the hero of the program. The Shadow had special insight into truth and human nature. Above all, the Shadow was the avenue to victory over evil! The Shadow, in other words, became part of the healing process.

How do we deal with the shadow? Whether in the nation, the group, or the individual, we deal with the dangers of the shadow and lift up its values by bringing it to our awareness and learning its message. Out of that shadow will come something either creative or demonic. Which of the two emerges will depend on what we do with it.

Jung has called to our attention that the shadow, the dark cloud in a dream, emerges from us as much as does the bright light of life. We need to acknowledge and own the shadow as ours. More, we must take seriously the lesson of the first chapter of Genesis. The Bible states that God created in the "darkness," and "It was good" (vs. 2). We need to see the shadow, then, as more than just a sign of human corruption. We need to see it as something that may contain a saving thrust. (Verses 16-18 tell us that God created light to rule over the darkness. The darkness thus needs to be managed, but it must not be ignored as without value or reality.)

I think of a therapist whose projection tests revealed a tremendous amount of inner anger. When confronted with this, the therapist said to the examiner, "The test is correct. I do have much inner anger, but I have learned to discipline myself. I understand the desire to kill so well that I have developed different ways of either controlling it or sublimating it. I seek to be sure that I do not get into situations that will push me beyond that control. I need to know that anger; but I also do not want to deny it. If I lose the capacity to be angry, I will let anyone walk over me."

One of the ways this person handled the anger was through humor. On one occasion, a hobo-type person approached him and asked whether he ever had killed anyone. Since the "hobo" had a reputation for being long-winded, the therapist could sense that he might have more on his hands than he could handle at that moment. So he replied, "No, I have never killed anyone, but I have often felt the urge to do so . . . and I feel that urge coming on right now." The hobo looked at him quizzically, laughed, and departed. Humor met both problems—the inner anger and the reality of the strangely dressed gentleman.

Those of us trained to be "always helpful and kind" may react against that response. Yet, on reflection, was it wrong? Therapists help people. Any time help is given, energy is expended. To conserve energy, the therapist must choose when to be expended, and when not. The shadow side of this therapist, which he recognized, allowed for him to survive—and to protect himself.

For the record, that particular therapist had held a pressure position for twenty-six years. Most of his predecessors had lasted only four or five years. Attention to and proper use of the shadow side of his life had made the difference.

On other occasions, the shadow side of life may in fact be demonic. The shadow may express itself in an act of murder, rape, molestation. In such an instance, the shadow side of strength is its use for evil.

Earlier, I spoke of the shadow as a dimension of light. The shadow works both passively and actively. Passively, someone or something stands in the way of light so that one cannot see. Actively, the shadow is a creative part of the light. In fact, without the shadow, the light would have no glory. An analogy is the double rainbow.

The double rainbow has several characteristics. Note that the colors in one rainbow appear in reverse order in the other. Note also that between the two rainbows, there appears a dark section greater than the darkness on the outside. That observation is no illusion. The darker middle section is called the Alexander belt, for the person who identified and studied it. This dark central belt functions in a way fundamental to the development of the double rainbow.

According to Dr. Alexander, in that dark belt a refraction occurs, which literally takes the light of the first rainbow and creates out of it the colors of the second rainbow. As in a prism, the colors are reversed. The black belt acts. In the rainbow shadow, dynamic action takes place to produce the new colors.

Does not this analogy give us much to think about when we speak of being in "the light of Christ"? Is it not possible that conversion, in Christ, can be understood more fully from this analogy than from the legalistic analogies developed from Jewish and Roman law? More important, as people who facilitate healing, I suggest that here we have an image of the healer as a part of the black belt, in which the one to be healed is transformed and emerges with new light. The creative suffering in the black belt becomes, for me, a model of the creative suffering in the healer. Out of that suffering, a new rainbow of health emerges in the healed.

When we remember, as we shall say again in the next chapter, that to speak of being created in God's image means to be created in God's shadow, surely we must see the importance of understanding the shadow in ourselves in order to understand ourselves as healers.

From physicists, then, we learn that the Alexander belt, far from being passive, both acts and creates. The creative work leads not only to light, but to light of beauty and color. We must understand the shadow as a place for considerable and important work. The work creates a new symbol which grows out of the shadow and makes real what happened in the shadow (in the case of the Alexander belt, the new rainbow). Let us call this work symbol work. This symbol work makes real what is there; without that work, what is there would not be real to us.

As we recall the importance of symbols, we come again to a sense of suffering and the role of suffering in the healing process. That is to say, suffering work has at its center symbol work, and symbol work relates to the formation of symbols. In the rainbow, the colors become symbols that grow out of the symbol work.

I see this model of the double rainbow as suitable for understanding the nature of the shadow. The view of the shadow as just the blocking of light is too passive and negative for either accuracy or understanding. The rainbow model may not carry the full sense of what takes place in the shadow. However, the model and the analogy show that the shadow must be understood as a dynamic experience within the psyche of each of us. Out of that shadow come creative new insights, a new wholeness of being, and symbols which give expression to and make real the new wholeness.

This view does not deny that the result of the shadow may be demonic and destructive. The acting out may go the wrong way. The task of the suffering healer, however, includes developing awareness of the shadow within, so that its lessons can be learned, its dangers can be avoided, and its positive work within the healer can give *freedom* for providing genuine care. Some may view freedom as weakness because it allows for evil (God's tragic flaw!). On the contrary, freedom is the opportunity for strength—strength even to suffer.

We must therefore move beyond the view that sees the shadow side of freedom as weakness, and say, "No, the shadow side of freedom is suffering." The capacity to suffer allows strength to be expressed in growth rather than in brutality. To have that opportunity means true freedom. The difference between growth and brutality depends on what we, as individuals or as groups, decide to do with the battle.

As healers, we need freedom in order to maintain our own inner capacity to suffer. Put biblically, this shadow side of freedom is the willingness to endure. In the book of Revelation, the letters to the seven churches contain the recurring theme, "To the one who endures, I will give the crown." The shadow side of freedom, then, is to go through the struggle of the Alexander belt—the pain of refraction, as it were—so that the new life of many colors may be created. We call such enduring neither weakness nor madness, but strength. As healers, we must endure.

On a couples' retreat, one of the spouses had a breakdown.[4] The behavior reflected itself in bizarre actions—a coffee cup thrown at the window; the announcement, "I am Jesus Christ." These actions caused considerable consternation and discussion.

At prayer time, the leader had developed a creative approach to the Bible; but the venture fell flat.

Why? The intervention in the form of devotions had no relation to the upset in the group *or* in the leader. The leader—or care giver—had provided a form of intervention (worship), but had not considered the shadow side of the group's experience. Nor had he looked at the shadow in himself. The focus was on the presentation, not on the shadow work, which was telling him that he must suffer the loss of a wonderful idea in order to meet the group where the group found itself—angry and upset over the psychotic upset.

The next day, the same group gathered for an evaluation. The person who had exhibited the strange behavior had gone for a walk. By now, the leader had had a chance to think things through and plan. Before the evaluation, he went to every person in the group and asked one simple question: "How do you feel?" In each instance, the response led to a sharing of feelings over the incident. Feelings of anger and guilt stood out. Some felt angry over the interruption; others felt guilty about their feelings. Some people felt both.

After talking with people individually, the leader had them all sit in a circle and asked if they wanted to discuss the experience. Feelings and thoughts poured forth. Some asked for an explanation. "What had happened?" "Could this happen to us?" "What really was going on?" One in the group had the background to speak about manic-depressive behavior—its causes and implications. Another was able to reflect on what the experience had taught him about himself and what it had suggested about the group.

When the person in question returned to the group, the bizarre behavior continued, but the group and the leader survived. Out of the experience, a new sense of community emerged. New strength developed as the members of the group discovered they could handle the strange actions.

In looking at this instance, we see that both the leader and the group as a whole had healing roles. In order to help, both the group and the leader had to deal with the shadow in themselves. I believe the person expressed that shadow. Who has not sometimes wished for the freedom to throw a cup at the wall, or through the window, or at the waiter—or even at the pastor, the doctor, the parishioner, the patient? What spouse has not at some time wished to express frustration, if not anger, at a husband or wife—and not known how to do it? Most of us simply repress those feelings, putting them aside as inappropriate. The fact is, to act on such feelings may be inappropriate, but to have such feelings is simply that—a fact, not a moral issue.

In any group on retreat, all those feelings are present. They are hidden in the individual shadows of each person. As the group becomes a group—a group person, as it were—those individual feelings become part of the larger group. They become part of the group shadow.

Whether the person was acting out the shadow as experienced, or merely bringing to light the group shadow that was present, makes little difference. The shadow existed. It could either become destructive and end the group or lead to a greater strength. Because the leader and the group worked with the shadow, the latter possibility resulted.

Yet, note that this healing took place only because the leader, as healer, and the group, as healer, allowed for their own suffering work. At the first meeting, the leader had stayed with a prearranged plan. He had not allowed himself to suffer loss of that plan or to recognize the shadow—either his own or that of the group. After that meeting, however, he did just that.

He sensed the need to look at the shadow within, to deal with what had come to awareness, and to learn from it.

Out of that look at the shadow, the leader found freedom to enter into the suffering with the group. He could raise with them the questions of the group shadow—"Could this happen to us? What does this say about us?" As they then became aware of the shadow, dealt with the suffering caused by the behavior, and endured, they found a new strength. They found a capacity to be a healing group for their friends and for the person with the bizarre behavior.

This case study also leads us to see that the creativity was not only in the shadow, but also in the way of dealing with the shadow. Being unaware of the shadow or denying its existence could have destroyed everything. The shadow might have asserted itself in its own form of bizarre group behavior. There could have been scapegoating. There could have been estrangement of the family. Either would have been demonic. Instead, out of the process of awareness, there came new support. Not unlike the second part of the double rainbow, there emerged the "many splendored thing" that love is.

Does this not take us back to our biblical roots and, at the same time, push us forward in our understanding of God and of suffering—and of the suffering healer? Some suggest that Judas represented the shadow side of Jesus. I think Peter did, as well. Surely Jesus would have liked to "buy off" the authorities as Judas did. Look at his experience of the temptations (Luke 4:1-13). The devil was part of that experience. The temptations were temptations simply because it would have been nice to be able to turn stones to bread, or possess the power of the legions of Rome, or have all worship him.

How demonic the shadow can be! The healer, whether Jesus or one of us, may well wish that with a prayer, he or she might have the power to cure, solve a problem, answer every question. How nice it would be if we could call down the presence of Christ on every issue that bothers us and have it solved. Yet even that desire can be a temptation of the devil and not an act of faith.

Jesus understood this dimension. He did not ignore the shadow, but owned its reality and faced it. Thus when Judas was paid, Jesus simply said, "What you are going to do, do quickly" (John 13:27). Jesus understood the depths that betrayal could reach, and he rejected it. He was prepared to endure, to suffer. He chose to suffer and give the suffering work the opportunity for a victory far beyond even the awful pain of Judas' betrayal.

Similarly, when Jesus told the disciples that he must go to the cross, Peter "began to rebuke him." Jesus had to reply, "Get behind me, Satan! For you are not on the side of God" (Mark 8:33). The capacity to heal means that the healer must have the capacity to suffer—to endure the shadow side of strength. For as we look at Jesus—whether beside Pilate or anyone else—Jesus is the one who emerges as truly strong. His is the strong name.

We therefore have the suffering of the cross. Yet, what is the cross? Is it not the cosmic Alexander belt of God? Is the cross not the place where Jesus enters into the problem of evil—the shadow in all of life—and endures, so that out of that struggle can come the healing?

In the Bible, there first came creation. God then gave the gift of freedom. Freedom gave the capacity for evil. Evil arrived on the scene. Then along came Jesus.

Some said of him, "He is not so much, otherwise he could save himself" (Mark 15:31, paraphrased). Yet, had he saved himself, had he withdrawn from the experience of the shadow, he would have been irrelevant. Instead, Jesus stayed with the struggle to its completion—his death. When the struggle was over, the soldier at the foot of the cross—we may presume he knew power when he saw it—said, "This was the Son of God" (Matt. 27:54).

Out of the black Alexander belt of the cross, out of the shadow of the cross, came the transformation in the bright colors of a new creation.

When, then, we see suffering in light of the shadow:

1. We learn that part of our intervention must be to stand with people so that they may have the courage not to give up the struggle that takes place in the shadow.
2. We learn that medication may surely be given, drugs may surely be taken (including alcohol), but that medication must not take away the individual's dignity in suffering the creative moment of the shadow. That creative moment leads to new life.
3. We see that part of the intervention is, in fact, to have that sense of presence which allows the healer to understand the nature of the struggle as others go through it. It is as others sense something of the meaning of the struggle that they then find a basis for being and the strength to be healed. To rob people of that opportunity is to rob them of healing. Yet to allow others to go through that struggle carries its own suffering—the suffering that is required of the healer.
4. We see that the question, "Why do bad things happen to good people?" is not the real question. The issue is not "Why does God let this happen?" The real

issue is that God wishes for us the ultimate experience of being truly creative. That experience must include the darkness—the shadow. That is the way we were created. That experience requires the opportunity for free will. The opportunity for free will in the universe requires the possibility of evil. The very existence of evil—of the demonic—is the evidence of God's greatness and love. The shadow is a gift of grace.

No, the reality of pain and the presence of evil are not evidence against God, but evidence for the ground of all our living. Once again, we find that the reality of the cross is the evidence that when we suffer, God suffers with us. God is in the shadow. If God is in the suffering, too, how can we blame God? From a Christian standpoint, as God identified with us in Jesus, so must we identify with others. As healers, we must endure suffering with those whom we hope to heal. We must live with the shadow.

By way of summary, consider the two thieves on the crosses with Jesus. One made the mistake of blaming God. The other recognized the goodness of God—recognized that that goodness was with them on the rack! For him, the question was not "Why does God not save himself and others?" The real question was whether the suffering healer would suffer enough to allow the dynamic of the shadow experience to exert its full thrust. Thus his request was, "Jesus, remember me when you come into your kingdom" (Luke 23:42).

In this way, the thief identified with the full journey and potential of the shadow. He wished to identify with the one who identified with him in suffering, so that he could indeed identify with him in the healing—paradise.

Therein we have the model of all healing. That is why we who would heal must be "suffering healers."

Early in my ministry, I gave a talk to a group of Dakota Indians on the dynamics of forgiveness. One of them commented, "What you have said is Greek to me." I then recast the whole presentation. After the next talk, a member of that group caught a phrase I had used and put it into a cartoon. The cartoon showed the light of God causing the cross to cast a shadow which illumined a Dakota at the foot of the cross. The caption read, "The shadow of the cross is the light of God's forgiveness."

That caption has been the theme of the above words. Suffering as the shadow side of freedom means strength. We must not fear suffering, but understand it and allow for its work. Today, I would paraphrase the word of the Dakotas. I would say that the shadow of the cross is the suffering work of God.

For those of us who would be healers, we then must take up our crosses, help our patients-clients-parishioners to take up their crosses—help them, not in a false journey of masochism but in a constructive walk with Christ—to find that which transforms the moment of sickness into the new creation of health.

II

We may speak then of the suffering healer. We may also speak of the healed healer.

Much has been said, and with great benefit, of the wounded healer. Henri Nouwen's book by that title is both constructive and insightful.[5] The theme is based on a parable from the days of the Pharisees.

However, another parable of the wounded healer comes from the Greeks. In that parable, the one who heals takes into himself—or herself—the ills of another. The model is found also in the biblical story of Moses leading the people through the wilderness.

In that story, the people walk through the wilderness in danger of poisonous snakes. As they go, Moses is instructed to lift up a serpent on a staff. As the people look at the staff with the serpent, they will be protected. The poison of the dangerous snakes is drawn out by the snake that is lifted up (John 3:14; Num. 21:9). In the biblical story, Jesus becomes the "suffering snake" on the staff who draws out the poison from those who will look.

The Greek myth comes in several forms.[1] Basically, the wounded healer is Aesculapius, who sometimes is represented as a snake. In one account, Apollo unites with Coronis, who gives birth to a child, Aesculapius. She exposes the child on Mt. Tithion, which is famous for medicinal plants. Here, Chiron, a centaur, teaches Aesculapius about healing. Chiron is a wounded physician. He is a Greek god, yet he suffers an incurable wound. His nature combines both animal and Apollonian aspects. Aesculapius takes on those qualities that make up his father, Apollo, and his adopted father, Chiron.

Chiron's wound is from a poisoned arrow. Aesculapius (the snake) is able to cure this wound in others, but for some reason, Chiron must keep the wound forever. The mystery—seen as a reality—is that the healer is able to heal only to the degree that there is a perpetual relationship to the wound that must be healed.

From this myth we may sense a truth that all who heal are wounded healers. The pastor who is open to others takes on the wounds of others. The doctor who loses energy during surgery has become tired not merely because of the operation, but has taken into himself/herself some of the suffering. The investment of a nurse in a patient while treating a wound is similar. Carl Jung's own doctor ministered to him when Jung suffered a heart attack. Jung recovered, but the doctor died after a heart attack. That instance of a physician dying of the disease he sought to cure is not an isolated one. Is that simply irony? Or is it possible that in some degree the myth is correct? Perhaps physicians take unto themselves the wounds they are able to cure; and the very carrying of those wounds allows the capacity for curing.

The Apostle Paul has a further insight. Paul understands suffering—enduring—as having to do not just with the pain of others but also with the euphoria of others. In counseling, clients often pour out all their feelings and then suddenly become happy at the end of the interview. It is not surprising for a person who has confessed a sin to a priest to walk out of the confessional with a new lightness—a new spring in the step. He shouts; she laughs. The release of pressure and the sense of freedom bring about that euphoria.

The counselor or the priest knows that the person is not yet fully healed. The euphoria may be as much a reaction to the release of poison from the wound as the pain was a reaction to the poison itself, but the release is not evidence that there has been a full cure.

However, if counselors or priests are to help their patients—confessants—they must be able to take into themselves the euphoria as well as the wound. Thus Paul writes that we must learn to "rejoice with those who rejoice, weep with those who weep" (Rom. 12:15). The healer must affirm the moment of joy as greatly as the moment of pain.

Suffering healers, then, do more than take into themselves a sense of the wound. They also take into themselves the release.

This insight pushes us to an understanding of the helper in the delivery of care that goes beyond the wounded-healer concept. Consider the various reactions to a wound: In order to protect against a wound, a care giver may build an impregnable wall. Some doctors, for example, seek to act purely as scientists—objective operators, removed from the patient. When, however, that wall of protection is broken, there is trouble. In a crisis moment, the wall has value in protecting the doctor's ability to function. We want that ability. We do not want the doctor to lose it. That moment of the "great technician" is real. Nevertheless, when the objective-distant doctor becomes the model for all physicians, there follows the process of treating diseases, not people. Such a model leads to the oft-stated instances when the disease was cured but the patient died.

Therefore, the impregnable-wall response to the wound in the healer does not work. The response fails when the wall is broken, for it leads to the complete collapse of the healer. The response fails because it does not truly heal—it only alleviates a particular crisis.

But when the counselor or physician loses all objectivity and totally identifies with the client or patient, we have the opposite of the wall response. In the moment of total identity, the healer fuses with the wounded. The fusion is so great, so all encompassing, that nothing is left for anyone else. Here, the care giver is not sufficiently removed from the problem. Here, the care giver becomes so consumed with the wounds of others that nothing is left for family, or even for self.

These instances of the "wall" and "identification" indicate ways in which demonic suffering becomes the problem of the care giver—the healer. In both instances, the healer does have a wound. Yet, in both instances, the response leads to the destruction of the healer. That destruction may be a breakdown, burn out, death. We do not need that kind of wounded healer.

We do need the healed healer. Whereas the healed healer has developed the capacity to suffer, the wounded healer may well have not. Suffering means there has been an enduring of the wound so that the wound no longer controls. It no longer is destroying the real soul. To paraphrase Luther's "The body they may kill, God's truth abideth still": "The wound may do its worst, the bond of death is burst." True healing, true salvation, true wholeness do not mean elimination of the scar. True healing means triumph over the effect of the wound.

The difference between a wound being gone and being no longer effective came through to me in the experience of my father. He had tuberculosis in the days before there was medicine to cure the disease and underwent the surgery known as collapsing the lung. The lung was pulled away from the rib cage in such a way that the germ was trapped in a pocket and could not get out. The procedure worked. My father had some thirty-five years of life after the surgery and returned to a full and productive career as a professor at Stanford University. Years later when he died, the problem was age and heart, not tuberculosis.

In a sense, his experience demonstrated the reverse of curing the disease but losing the patient—the disease survived but the patient lived.

In counselors, pastors, social workers, physicians, we need, then, healers who not only know how to suffer, but whose suffering becomes the means of overcoming the wound and healing the individual. That person is either a suffering healer or a healed healer. The problem of pain in the world requires not so much the wounded healer, but the healed healer. The world needs not so much the wounded group, as the healed group.

The old saying, "Physician, heal thyself," comes from the view that one cannot heal another unless one has personally been healed. The sciences of personality have brought this view to the healing arts; it has not come from the medical model. It is in psychotherapy that one thing has become clear: If we who would heal are not to project our own neuroses, hopes, dreams on another, *we must have that healing* which allows us freedom to deal with the needs of others.

From all this, we see the healed healer as one who has (1) learned how to deal with a wound; (2) experienced healing; and, (3) in moving back and forth between being wounded and being healed, has become able to heal. For that reason a pastor or counselor needs another healer as a constant reference. The care giver must go to a care giver in order to deal with those personal inner wounds that could prevent touching the inner wound of another.

The pastor in Maugham's story was not able to deal with the needs of the prostitute because he had not dealt with the prostitute in himself. Had he had his own helper, who could have provided him with the space to look at that wound within himself, he could then have found the healing that would have allowed him truly to bring care to the prostitute.

We must add to the view of the suffering healer that of the healed healer. The healer must have that endured (suffered) wound in order to reach the wound in the wounded. However, the healer must also have that healing which frees one to bring healing to the one to be healed.

In this process, one does not do the healing. The healer only facilitates the process by which the healing takes place. Whether it is a doctor who puts two bones together so that they can grow or provides a medicine that allows the system to cope; a counselor who works with a depressed patient; a community caught in the ravages of a disaster—the care giver cannot really cure the situation. The care giver provides the dynamic in which the life-giving force may be at work. (Many of us see that life-giving force as God, but the point is true, even for those who do not).

The experience of the crucifixion pulls all this together. In the crucifixion, Jesus takes on the pain of all people. He takes on the pain of isolation from people and from God. He takes on the pain of meaninglessness. He takes on the pain of pain itself. Yet in all this, he does not "lose it." He does not "curse God and die." Through the experience of prayer, he learned to find that healing which allowed him not to deny himself. He was honest about the suffering ("I thirst"; "My God, my God, why have you forsaken me?"). He never denied his real self as a forgiving person ("Father, forgive them, they know not what they do.") He affirmed the wholeness, the healed aspect of who he was in relation to God ("Into thy hands I commend my spirit"; "It is completed.")[6]

The crucifixion thus resulted in the affirmation of a soldier ("Truly, this was the son of God.") and the view of many of us that he was fulfilling the statement of Isaiah, "By his stripes we are healed."

Out of this view, we have concluded that the suffering healer is not only a wounded healer but, equally important, a healed healer. If, out of this suffering experience, the wounded healer must also become the healed healer, the following steps must be identified. These have been drawn from conversations with a surgeon who does heart transplants, with a psychiatrist, a pastor, and a nurse, and from my own experience. Other supporting references may be found in biographies of Albert Schweitzer, Sir William Grenfell, Anne Morrow Lindbergh, and others.

1. Suffering healing requires professionalism, but a rejection of professional idolatry. In professional idolatry, we focus on the profession and on ourselves as the professionals, as though we had all the answers.

Professionals find it hard to say, "I need help." In counseling, for example, the professional counselor feels, "I am expert in this area. People come to me, I do not go to others. Why would I seek counseling?" People who indulge in this idolatry may be aware of the need of peer communication and attend many conferences, but they have a real problems with "I may be wrong."

The discussion of the shadow in the professional is indicative of this point. Only with the help of another do we find that check and balance against our own prejudices. Failure to look at the shadow shows itself in professional idolatry, in the wall of defense, in the raised voice, in the "I know the answer" mentality, and in the failure to listen creatively. This idolatry shows itself in the inability to deal with a mistake. The result is often denial, breakdown, destructive suffering.

True professionalism includes the capacity to suffer, to learn and grow, to know there is no situation from which learning cannot come, to know that any of us see only part of the total situation—whatever that situation may be.

We all need to know that our view of life is not unlike the word processor on which I am writing. At any one time, the screen will show a portion of this manuscript—but only a portion. I must learn to hit the right keys to see other parts. This machine has more "right keys" than I can remember. I have to know the resources. I have to ask others for help. I have to know that I will never know all the answers.

2. Suffering healing requires space for personal renewal. Earlier, I mentioned the model of Jesus Christ. Christ felt energy go out of him, took time for private meditation and prayer, and knew that he could not be sacrificed on every altar. "My time is not yet come," he said. Christ did not have to be God! He could leave things to God. Even in his high-priestly prayer, he said, "They are thine" (John 17:9). He could not do it all himself.

Christ thus stayed with God's process. That process included death and resurrection at the points where death and resurrection had to be. He said, "Let this cup pass from me. Nevertheless, not my will but yours be done." For Christ, the issue was not "Why does this happen?" For him, the issue was how to stay in the process—the process of life, God's process.

Christ allowed both himself and others to be part of the process. He could say to others, "Go to Jerusalem to pray" (be renewed yourselves and part of the process), and he could weep.

3. The suffering healer continues to practice the developmental task of letting go. That is simply grief work; but it encounters pain. It is living out all that was said in an earlier chapter about letting go. In the example of the leader and the man with the strange behavior, we see the importance of "letting go." Had the leader not acted as he did, the constructive work with the congregation would never have taken place. Had he focused on the way he handled the group in the mountains, or had he wallowed in grief, his ability as a care giver would have ended. The letting go in suffering work made the difference.

A patient dies. What do physicians and pastors do with that experience? I do not mean just with the death of the body of someone—but that part of them in the other person that must be buried; that part of the other person in them that must be let go. If a pastor cannot make progress with a client, how does that pastor handle the referral? Does one refer and just forget, as a form of denial, or does one refer and allow for follow-up? Such referral may remind us that we do not have all the answers. Again, one must suffer the pain of that reality. Care givers must also allow themselves and their clients to realize that referral does not mean rejection.

4. Suffering healing allows not for the *window* of vulnerability but for the *risk* of vulnerability. So much is said these days about defense and closing the "window of vulnerability" that we miss the point of the risk. The risk of vulnerability is part of the process of healing. That point, often forgotten by defense department officials, too often also goes unrecognized by those who would bring care. Whether a doctor is risking a patient's infection or a counselor is risking a client's wrath, if not outright attack, there is a risk of vulnerability in all healing.

Even more, the model of the healed healer demands that risk. In the servant model and in the person-on-the-cross model, Jesus took that risk and commanded it for others (John 12). One part of that risk means not dumping one's feelings on the client. It means a people not acting out their anger on another people. It means not inappropriately exposing oneself and one's problems to a group or to a client. Above all, it means the risk of being available to pain.

Expressed positively, the risk of vulnerability means allowing what Martin Buber called the I-Thou relationship.[7] (I would add that it means equally allowing for the I-I or the Thou-Thou relationship.) In the I-Thou relationship, people experience one another as people. Professionally, it means allowing others to relate to care givers as people—not just as professionals who are upholding an image. Insistence on the image reduces everyone to the level of an "it." This I-Thou relation means knowing how to recognize transference and deal with it. Too often, a client or a supervisor experiences a feeling of falling in love with the other person. There are ways of dealing with that transference. It is as important to maintain the separateness of individuality throughout the I-Thou relationship as to allow for a good feeling of love.

The I-I has to do with those moments when one sees oneself as one is—hurting or happy, fulfilled or fragmented. Dr. Peck, in his *People of the Lie,* gives a good example of the I-I relationship.[8] In the counseling room, a client told Dr. Peck that he had made a pact with the devil to sell his child. Dr. Peck was so stunned he was silent. The patient asked for a response. At that moment, Dr. Peck recognized that he himself needed help. In some respect, he had become a patient, too, but the client clearly was not the one to help him.

Replied Dr. Peck, "I am not ready to respond."

In that moment of counseling, the I-I was at work in Dr. Peck. He allowed himself to be himself and, out of that, acted appropriately to who he was. As a result, he was able to move through the experience and deal with the patient in front of him.

In the Thou-Thou relation, the counselor allows two people to experience a relationship with each other. This is seen often in marriage counseling. In the midst of the struggle, the husband and wife may suddenly have a moment of true personal encounter. The Thou-Thou comes alive because of the context the counselor has provided.

Each of these moments is a risk. The moment of being a true person may be violated by another. Yet, without willingness to suffer that risk, there will never be health or healing.

5. Finally, the suffering-healing requires worship and surrender to victory.

Worship does not receive the attention it deserves in many areas of the pastoral-care field. Yet historically, the dynamic of the worship experience has had a critical place. Too easily, we dismiss the injunction of Jesus to the cleansed lepers that they show themselves to the priests (Luke 17). We see it as simply fulfilling an ancient temple regulation, rather than as lifting up the role of symbolizing the fact of cleansing, return to the community, surrender to victory.

The liturgy of worship provides numerous areas of help in suffering work. At the outset, it provides space. One person in a discussion group said, "I go to church, for there no one can get to me." The comment was not cynical. Rather, that person found that the liturgy, the music, the time for focus on the Scripture, the time to pray, gave him space for renewal. Often religious care givers become so involved in the mechanics of religious work that their own need for the "space" of worship vanishes.

The service of worship also provides a time when all present may search for effective symbols. Luther supposedly held that the liturgy should be rewritten every two years. I heard Karl Barth say that every generation should rewrite the creed in its own language. Both Luther and Barth therefore hold up the need for individuals to find the language, the symbols, which deal with the process of suffering work and the surrender to victory (affirmation of faith). Exposition of Scripture in the sermon, when done with a view to interpretation, helps the listener sense the symbols of the past and discover the symbols of the present. Prayer gives opportunity for recognizing the shadow side of life and for moving on to affirmation of the victories in the midst of shadows.

In group worship, it is the responsibility of the leader to help the group as a whole become aware of its shadows and its suffering work, and the symbol work inherent in both.

In and of itself, the liturgy also becomes a model of the suffering work. The period of confession lifts up a time when, as a group, and privately as individuals, confrontation with the dark side begins. If the reading of the Scripture and the sermon follow the confession, that look at the shadow may deepen, or a move may begin toward praise and joy. The result may be restlessness or upset, on one side, or excitement and uplift, on the other. If prayers follow the sermon, the move in either direction continues in a way that leads to surrender—surrender to the reality of either the shadow's message or the victory. Thus, in and of itself, the time of worship may symbolize the whole dynamic of suffering work.

Worship means different things to different people. Worship may be the traditional act of adoration. For others, it may be the time of privacy, the moment of self-evaluation, or the occasion for a sense of being part of a fellowship.

Whatever the meaning of worship, I feel that for each of us, the suffering-healing dynamic requires some form of spiritual leader. There must be someone who can help each of us look at the shadow, see what the shadow is saying to us, and integrate that wisdom. There must be someone who can also help us take the time to look at the light and find that brightness which the dark cannot take away.

Suffering-healing is a process that leads to a realized creation in the life of each of us. Elsewhere, I have related this experience of a new creation to the dynamic of forgiveness.[9] The discovery of this new creation in ourselves takes time. Yet that discovery, once made, justifies the effort and the suffering. It is an experience above "all that we ask or think" (Eph. 3:20).

CHAPTER VI

Symbols, Scripture, and Strategy

The Bible may be used in two ways with those who suffer: as a source of understanding and as a means of ministry. Many use the Bible for study. Too few understand its value devotionally.

In the preceding chapters, we have used the Bible in both ways. I have sought to allow for a dialogue between experience with the Bible as an object of understanding and experience with the Bible as part of the healing process. Now the time has come to pull together our thoughts on suffering and an understanding of the role of symbols in dealing with suffering. In so doing, we must look at symbols and how they work, at the Bible and how it helps us find symbols, and finally, at the strategies for intervention which grow out of this discussion.

I

Symbolization is part of the healing process—part of the way we become whole. Symbol work is part of suffering work.

Contribution to the understanding of symbols has come to us from the field of psychiatry in the works of Freud and Jung, and from the fields of philosophy and theology in the works of Whitehead and Tillich. Others, such as Susan Langer, have built on the insights of those people in helpful and most creative ways.[1] A symbol is more than a sign that points the way. A symbol helps make alive that to which it is pointing. Susan Langer suggests that the great leap on the sixth day of creation brought about the difference between humans and animals—the capacity to symbolize.

The word *table,* for example, does not look like a table. Yet when we use the word we know exactly what we mean. And without the word, we cannot communicate the idea of a table. The very naming of the table gives us a basis for using it, managing it, dealing with it—without a table being always present.

The importance of this ability became clear in one of the interviews mentioned previously. When Fred spoke with Joseph about AIDS despite fear of the subject, they found that increased understanding of the disease helped them. Said Fred, "I discovered that naming the beast itself was a means of managing the beast."

The book of Revelation is full of symbols that seek to "name the beast." The book did not change the pain. The book did not give a weapon for stopping the persecution. Yet naming the beast itself became a means of dealing with the beast, of putting the beast into manageable proportions (13:18).

The book of Revelation names not only the beast, but the victory. If we were to take the last chapters and reduce them to signs that give us a road map to heaven, we would miss the strength of the book. It describes evil being thrown into the sea and says, "there was no more sea" (21:1). That portrays a symbol of victory over evil far more than a literal throwing of a bag into the ocean. A description of the "new Jerusalem" is far more than a tourist guide to get one around a temple square. In fact, there is no temple. We find God. The description brings alive the victory—the reality—more than any road map.

The church in the first five centuries dealt with symbols. The various ecumenical councils developed great confessions of faith which represented more than documents to be signed by opposing groups. These confessions expressed the corporate, creative growth of the people. The very confessions of Nicaea, or Chalcedon, or Constantinople were the process by which the oneness became effected. In those days they were not called confessions of faith, but "symbols of the church." They were not directives to the true church. They were statements which helped the true church come alive.

When Karl Barth said that each generation needed to write its own creed, he identified the truth that each generation needs to find its own symbol of meaning.

Symbol work, then, is getting a handle on whatever is taking place and seeking, with that handle, to deal with that event.That symbol not only points to the reality but also reflects the reality, and is itself part of the reality being reflected. A diagnosis, for example, becomes a symbol to the degree that it not only tells us what a disease is and what must be done to treat the disease; it also helps us get hold of the disease and deal with its effect upon each of us. Diagnosis creates understanding. We can cope with what we understand far better than with what we do not understand.

A number of years ago I received a call from a client whose dog had died. The client was terribly distressed. He could not deal with the grief, and he could not understand his degree of difficulty. As he talked, we spoke of the fact that his father had died a year earlier. During that experience, the client had been rational, controlled, "on top of things." But the death of the dog had opened up all those beautifully controlled feelings. Now the client had to deal not only with grief over his dog, but also grief over his father.

Awareness of these two aspects did not remove the grief. It did, however, bring him a sense of relief. He could say, "That's true; I have a right to feel upset." The diagnosis became a symbol that pointed to the healing that was needed, and itself was a part of the healing.

The task of intervention, then, in any suffering—group or individual—includes help with the process of symbol work. People need help in finding those symbols that will allow the suffering work to take place. The symbol work is necessary for the suffering work.

II

The Bible itself helps us find symbols that work. Consider those who wrote the Bible and the matter of the Exile experience.

The Exile took place about 587–538 B.C. The Hebrews went as captives to Babylonia. In Exile, the people had to make sense out of what had happened to them. The development of the books of Kings and Chronicles and the use of the Pentateuch became means of "naming" the disaster and the triumph of God's judgment. Kings shows both the shadow of the group and the rainbow. Psalms brings to awareness symbols of both the confrontation with evil and the victory over it (e.g., Psalm 51, mentioned earlier). The tasks of writing and using these books became a means of symbolizing—of making real—the experience of the past and the experience of God.

Reading the law had the same effect. The law, especially in the form of Deuteronomy, helped to symbolize the view of God that should be rejected and lift up the view that should be accepted. That book helped the Jews find symbols for teaching and living.

As we read the Bible, we must sense what the symbols are bringing alive. One must identify whether the symbol relates to an individual or to a group. When the passage says, "How long, O Lord, wilt thou forget thy people?" we have a symbol that deals with corporate suffering. When Jesus says, "Father, forgive them," again the suffering intervention is corporate. When, however, Jesus says, "Father, let this cup pass from me," or the psalm says, "The Lord is my shepherd," the issue is individual suffering.

Further, the Bible makes a distinction between individual sin and the battle against cosmic evil. The two are related, but there is a difference. Often in Scripture, the individual is saying, "What have I done wrong?"

That is the lesson of Job. His friends assumed that because Job was suffering, he had done something wrong. Job was honest enough not to sell out for less than what was true.

The issue for Job was not his sin, but the battle against a cosmic evil. Job suddenly saw the difference. When God asks, "Where were you when I laid the foundation of the earth?" (38:4) and goes on to say, "Can you draw out leviathan with a fishhook?" (41:l), Job is receiving a symbol. The symbol brings alive to him that the issue is not personal but cosmic. He, Job, has done nothing wrong. He, Job, is part of the cosmic battle in which God is engaged. Job sees this and cries out, "I have heard of thee by the hearing of the ear: but now mine eye seeth thee."

Job's confession then becomes its own symbol—a symbol of the triumph of his relation with God. The symbol makes real his surrender to victory. It is then that Job copes with the pain. It is then that he sees the meaning in his suffering which allows him to suffer.

On other occasions in the Bible, the issue is one of guilt for a specific sin. David suffers in the death of his firstborn son because of the sin. He recognizes this, and thus when the sin is handled through the death, he does not wallow in the suffering. He moves on. Psalm 51 dealt with this matter of individual guilt and sin. Both the woman caught in adultery and the prodigal son are examples of dealing with individual guilt.

In the Bible, there are four words translated by the English *suffering*:

Aphiemi has to do with the idea of letting something go. When Jesus says, "Suffer little children . . . to come unto me" (Matt. 19:14), he means that others must let them go.

The word has within it the idea of rending or tearing. It is a word that applies to grief work—whether that grief has to do with letting children go off to school or to be married, or with surrendering one who has died. All the developmental stages discussed earlier relate to this word.

Pathema is the most familiar word for suffering. From it comes the English word *pathos*. This word has to do with suffering as a deep, profound feeling. The feeling may be neurotic or healthy. It may express lust or concern. When Jesus says that "the Son of man must endure many things," he is using the word in a healthy sense.

Epitrepo, though not often used, carries the implication of permission, as in "Suffer me to bury my parents."

Perhaps *pascho* comes down to us as the most famous word for suffering. It deserves special attention in this matter of finding symbols. When Jesus celebrated the Passover, he was observing the *pasch,* which has to do with the sacrificial lamb. In this sense, suffering meant sacrifice. Matthew and Mark make heavy use of this word. They knew the temple ritual. In that ritual, surrendering to suffering was seen as part of surrendering to the process of life—a surrender with confidence that the process ultimately led to victory. The Resurrection confirmed that confidence. As Paul said later, "If Christ be not raised [from the dead], we are of all men most miserable" (I Cor. 15:17, 19).

Pasch leads us to an understanding of the process of symbol work in the Bible. Earlier, I pointed out that when Abraham went to the mountain, his problem was not to avoid the suffering, but to find a way to deal with it. He discovered a symbol that did just that. The ram in the thicket became the symbol. He did not need to sacrifice his son. In the New Testament, Jesus now becomes that symbol.

This illustration suggests that each of us goes to the mountain to seek a way of restoring our relationship with God. We want to be rid of the sins we have committed—or at least of the effect of them. However, we cannot do that alone. To the degree that Jesus can become a symbol of the process, the suffering work around our own sins takes place. We deal with the sin and can move on.

Jesus also had a sense of being part of the battle against cosmic evil. He said, "I saw Satan fall like lightning from heaven" (Luke 10:18). To the degree that we, like Job, find that we must suffer for evil that is not of our making, Jesus again can become the symbol. We need the symbol work that allows Jesus to make the victory real for us.

From a corporate standpoint, the Jews have found that symbol in the Seder. In the Seder, the Passover meal, the *pasch* has the central place. The Seder is celebrated by almost all Jews—whether they are pious, devout, atheistic. Practiced by family after family, the Seder has helped keep the Jewish nation alive and healthy as a people, down through the centuries of persecution and turmoil.

Before the Seder, the house has been cleaned and all has been prepared. The mother lights the candles. Each food on the table has its meaning, and as the meal progresses, someone—usually the oldest son—asks specific questions dealing with the Exodus. The story of liberation and freedom is told as the meaning of each food item is explained.

The meal identifies with more than just history. It looks also to the future—to Elijah's return and to the promise of the Holy Land. "Next year at this time, may this meal be celebrated in Jerusalem," is the prayer. Thus the meal becomes a symbol of liberation, of victory, of hope.

When Jesus met with his disciples, he knew what was about to happen. He took that Passover meal—that *pasch*—and invested it with new meanings to help provide the symbols that could allow for the suffering his death would cause. The bread and the cup were no longer the unleavened bread of the Exodus or the blood on the doorposts of the Hebrew homes. Rather, the bread and the wine became "my body" and "my blood." That supper in Jerusalem was no longer just a geographical matter but had become a cosmic one—"I will no longer share this feast with you until I share it with you in the banquet feast of my father's kingdom" (Matt. 26:29, paraphrased).

Thus the New Testament itself becomes a means of seeking those symbols and helping with the symbol work that will allow people to do their suffering work—regardless of the issue. The Resurrection gives us a great demonstration of symbol work. We do not know how the Resurrection took place. We do know that it makes the victory on the cross real. The Resurrection of Christ became, for the disciples, and becomes for us, the logical expression of Christ's surrender to the victory over evil. The task for us becomes one of knowing how we also can surrender to that victory.

If, as suffering healers or as healed people, we now understand life in the context of that Resurrection and that victory, how does that understanding happen? How does that symbol come alive for us? The Bible gives two specific approaches:

One approach, in the experience of Thomas, speaks of finding as direct an awareness as possible of the risen Christ. Jesus appears and Thomas is told to "put your finger here and see my hands; put out your hand, and place it in my side" (John 20:27). Jesus appears on the road to Emmaus and breaks bread with the disciples (Luke 24). Jesus tells Mary not to grasp him because now she must see him in a different way (John 20:17). Paul has a vision and seeks to make that vision real to others (Acts 9). Rituals are suggested (John 21). All these instances suggest ways in which people may sense the victorious Christ. That awareness can then enable them to cope with the suffering moment.

The second approach suggests meditation and prayer. The disciples are told to go to Jerusalem until the Holy Spirit comes upon them (Luke 24:49). Paul speaks of the Holy Spirit and what that means for daily life. The daily-life practice thus becomes part of the symbol that allows one to do the suffering work (e.g.,

I and II Cor.). The Letter of James speaks about the life of faith—the life that gives expression to the victory. The First Letter of Peter speaks of suffering as education. All these statements help people find symbols that, in a time of extreme pain and suffering, allow them to make the triumph real and deal with what must be suffered.

The book of Revelation puts both approaches together. It begins with the concept of prayer and meditation—"I was in the Spirit on the Lord's Day" (1:10)—and goes on to portray in different symbols that reality of Christ as victorious—"I saw . . . one like unto the Son of man" (Rev. 1:13).

The Bible thus records how people found symbols that worked and allowed the suffering work to take place—both individually and corporately. The Bible is a tool we can use to find those symbols that will allow us the same capacity to suffer that was true of those who wrote it.

Unfortunately, people sometimes reduce the events of the Bible to signs that give false expectations. That practice leads to disastrous results. In another context, Jesus said, "This generation . . . seeks a sign, but no sign shall be given to it" (Luke 11:29). Jesus used the statement in reference to those who would seek proof that the end of the world was at hand and the new Kingdom was to be ushered in. The warning fits our time and subject, too. In the Bible, we are dealing with dynamic and living symbols that allowed for suffering work. That suffering work carried through to a victory. A reduction of the symbolic life of the Bible to rituals, or forms, or signs simply destroys the dynamic life of the Bible.

As we move now to a summary of the forms of intervention in suffering, we must be sure that what we do allows the process to work and does not simply mimic a process of the past. The former allows for strength and coping. The latter leads only to illusion and disillusion.

III

Now we come to strategy. The conclusion of our study responds to this issue: "Define the Christian strategy in suffering." Individual strategy depends on the people at the scene. The previous pages have suggested tactics and specific techniques. Strategy has to do with the broad scope of an intervention. Given these guidelines, each of us, as an individual, must decide what to do and how to do it, in our own scene. Here we will refer back to the examples of Edith and the poverty-stricken village in India.

The first step in intervention centers on the focus of the suffering. With Edith, the focus was individual; with the village, the focus was group. Despite appearances, no issue is purely individual and no issue is purely corporate. Yet there is a focus that makes difference.

If the focus proves clearly individual, then the cluster of related issues must be identified. Without awareness of the cluster or of the system of relations that form the suffering experience, intervention will be unproductive and frustrating.

For Edith, that cluster involved separation from students, the death of her own body, the need to come to terms with events, and the need to deal with the hospital. In relation to each, she identified the need to have meaning in her death. She said of her funeral, "I want this to be a statement."

For the village, the system involved the economic and health structures of both the small community and the larger society. The system also demanded a means of dialogue between the small community and the larger. The villagers therefore had to identify their own liaison with the outer world. The powers within the community had to be brought forth in order that the power of the social worker and the hospital could relate. Individual feelings and individual styles could not be ignored. The nurses had to talk with each person as an individual. Yet, those personal approaches had to be carried out with awareness of the impact on the group as a whole of any individual instruction, any individual help.

If the focus proves to be on a suffering group, then any appropriate intervention must differentiate between types of groups. A family in therapy forms one type of group. The dynamics of intervention there will be different from those in a school class that has just learned that one of its number has been killed—and they will be different from those in a congregation or a people.

From sharpening of the nature and focus of the sufferer, attention must turn to the healer. I believe the prime task of a healer is to stand with the suffering person or group in order to share the healing power. The power offered does not avoid the suffering but allows the suffering work to accomplish its goal of victory. Whether in the individual sufferer or the suffering group, I define the prime form of intervention as *empowerment—shared power* is the strategy. (Although first used during the war-on-poverty days in the 1960s, the social-service use of that term actually grew out of the leadership of the late Charles T. Leber of the former Board of Missions of the Presbyterian Church. Dr. Leber initiated the concept that missionary work could not be one of moving into a country as though the country or culture had nothing to offer. The missionary brought a power, but the country and culture also had power to offer. Hence, the name *missionary* was changed to *fraternal worker*. At the Community Service Society, we adopted this same attitude in 1970 when we formally established *shared power* as the foundation for moving into the depressed areas of New York City. The definition is my own.)

Shared power assumes that everyone has a power to share. In counseling, the therapist clearly has something to offer. However, so does the client. The power to receive care, for example, is itself a power. There are other powers a client may contribute—the power to pay, the power of a good mind, the power of knowledge of the nature of the suffering. The power to receive help is itself basic to the suffering process. In offering this power to the healer, the client shares a strength with the suffering healer.

The necessity of this power for receiving help means something for us as care givers. The suffering healer must also have the basis for being healed so that he or she may intervene appropriately. If the healer cannot receive what the wounded has to offer, the process of healing will be blocked. Intervention by a therapist that leads to dependency will not help. Intervention that is threatened by the idea that the care giver also needs care—and perhaps care from the recipient—also will fail. Shared power means that the social worker, pastor, counselor, must be aware of what he or she must receive as well as give.

For the individual care giver, this may mean the need of a therapist or peer group where evaluation can take place, where the helper's feelings can be handled, where growth can take place. For the group care giver (such as a medical team, a rescue group, a church), this need may mean a constant process of debriefing, of evaluation, of renewal.

The suffering healer must have a process of becoming the healed healer and of dealing with the suffering that comes from the intervention itself.

Shared power also means that the healer must seek and lift up the true powers of the individual or the group. Edith had theological knowledge, personal determination, an ability to make decisions, awareness of what she wanted. The role of the pastor included affirming those powers and doing those things that allowed them to function. The poverty-stricken village had young people with some ego strength and a capacity for humor, a woman who could be part of the group yet transcend the group's problems, a structure that allowed the group to hold together despite the poverty. The social worker helped to affirm those strengths and build on them.

In all suffering—group or individual—decisions must be made as to what can or should be done to eliminate the cause of the suffering. A caterpillar, in struggling to emerge from a cocoon, could have its pain alleviated by a helper who simply cut the cocoon. The result would be wings that did not have the strength to fly. Intervention by removing the cocoon would not be appropriate. But something else could happen—a sudden drop in temperature would cause death. Intervention by stopping the drop in temperature would be appropriate.

This issue of appropriate intervention must be faced—whether the question is one of giving drugs to a patient or a financial handout to a community. Dependency will destroy both the patient and the community—and maybe even the care giver. As indicated in the case of Edith, the guide is whether the physical intervention will aid the process of the suffering work or prevent it.

In both individual and corporate suffering, the care giver(s) must come to an understanding of the suffering and its meaning. It is the task of the healer(s) to lift up that understanding so that it can be "named." To the degree that the care giver acts professionally, the care giver does those things that allow for competence and growth. That growth includes letting go of the professional status for the sake of the process itself.

The healer(s) must take time for renewal.

The care giver(s) must take the risk of vulnerability.

The healer(s) must provide the opportunity for developing meaningful symbols that will allow the suffering work to take place.

In a group situation, work in the slums leads people to an awareness of a power not evident on the surface. In my own first years of working among depressed people, what caught my attention was not the tragedy of their lives, but their strength to carry on even in the midst of tragedy. It became evident that part of the immediate task of a care giver or a caring group was to identify the power the people did have.

Intervention, therefore, in the process of suffering work, requires a mutual empowerment. The power goes both ways—not just one way. That expectation requires a degree of humility on the part of the care giver.

There are, then, four categories of intervention in the suffering process: freedom to suffer, awareness, meaning, and symbolization.

1. The category of freedom to suffer involves the ability of the therapist to suffer with those who suffer. As God suffers when we suffer, so we suffer as others do. It is easier to give a person a pill in order to sleep than to suffer with the struggle. The freedom to suffer

involves the matter of shared power. If the care given truly empowers an Edith or a village in India, the care giver also feels the suffering of an Edith or a village in India. Freedom of power and freedom to empower are not possible without sharing the pain. Shared suffering will accompany shared power.

2. The matter of awareness involves consciousness-raising. To the degree that raising something to one's consciousness means also "naming the beast," this process relates to the matter of symbol work. Yet it is also different. Just because something is in one's awareness does not mean that one has made sense of it, has it under control, can cope. In fact, the very reason something is out of one's awareness may be the reason one has difficulty coping.

This consciousness-raising must be at the physical-emotional, the mental-intellectual, and the spiritual levels. Inability to feel pain, for example, will mean inability to feel pleasure. What deadens one deadens the other. Dead nerve endings are dead to hot and cold alike. Problems not brought to the mind's awareness will not be solved, because the questions have not been asked. The issue of good and evil, of true wholeness and true loss of life, will not be met where there is no self-consciousness.

Awareness, then, is a critical category, without which the freedom to suffer—and to accomplish the suffering work—will not take place.

3. The category of the search for meaning is both facilitated by care givers and contributed to by them. A care giver may have an insight that excites another when shared. In the midst of suffering work, an individual or group may suddenly come alive to a truth that puts the whole concern into perspective. Meaning is given and one can cope.

For instance, as someone asked, "Where is God?" when they saw the boy struggling on the gallows, from within Elie Wiesel came the response, "God is here on the gallows." He had the insight that came to him as a revelation and gave him a moment of meaning—a moment that allowed him to cope with the experience.

Years afterward, however, a group of people struggled with the suffering they endured. They could find no meaning. They found it hard to cope. Then, together, they read the story *Night*. As they came to the recounting of that experience, there was sudden silence. A look of recognition went around the circle. Wiesel's insight became their revelation. The meaning allowed them to make sense out of what was happening and to cope.

4. The category of symbol work might be described as one role for worship or meditation. There are other roles for worship and meditation. Those who lead in these functions miss an important dimension, however, if they do not understand the role of helping individuals or groups find symbols that work.

The experience of Bill in an earlier chapter demonstrates how one may help an individual find symbols. The process began by taking Bill "where he was." That starting point is the key. First there must be relaxation of the muscles. That is done by first tensing, then relaxing each muscle in the body. However, "where Bill was" included the pain around the incision in his back. The healer must know enough anatomy to avoid muscles that would only make the pain worse.

Discussion with Bill also identified where he was in his thought patterns. At that moment, guilt had no place. The issues of isolation and frustration did. Those were dealt with by the healer's seeking to communicate a continuing presence and the assurance of return visits.

Although I did not do this with Bill, it is wise to ask a person in advance, as the therapist asked me, "What is the most beautiful, peaceful spot you know?" In so doing, the healer avoids lost time while the person seeks that special place. The fact that the *person* picks the special spot must not be avoided, however. I would never have thought of Bill's living room. My mind was on the mountains. That living room and its contents had special meanings for Bill. The task was to allow him to find his own symbols and let the meanings come alive for him.

Similar points relate to group process. The sacrament of Communion has many meanings. Yet, these meanings may have been lost because a congregation as a whole has not come to find the symbols that are there for them. The service of worship may be conducted too quickly, too casually, without proper preparation. Once, every experience of Communion was preceded by a "preparatory service." In the Reformation tradition, every experience of the sacrament is to include a sermon that prepares the congregation. Too often, the relation between the sermon and the act of the sacrament is purely accidental or coincidental.

The close of a conference or group retreat may not seem to be the greatest example of suffering. Yet for some, closure is painful. At the end of one such week-long conference in which a group had shared much and become close, the act of departing was not easy. The leader brought the group together and placed in front of them coffee, tea, and crackers—all they had been accustomed to having at the daily coffee break. He then explained that when Jesus was helping the disciples find symbols that would work for them, he used what was already familiar—the elements of the Seder, or Passover meal.

"So," said the leader, "we take what has become familiar to us—the cups of coffee and tea, and the crackers." He then went through a paraphrase of the Communion service. Then each person served the next person. In the process, the fact of the separation was lifted up, the intent to stay together in the common purpose of ministry was affirmed, and prayer was shared by the group.

The process did not end the pain, but it did result in a sense of peace about the break. The suffering work led to an ability to move on, let go of the past, and return to the various places of ministry.

The category of symbol work has many expressions. Whether in the group or in the individual, part of the task of intervention is to allow for finding those symbols.

IV

I sum up the whole strategy in this way: Suffering cannot be averted. The issue is to move from demonic suffering to creative suffering. Demonic suffering leads to the destruction not only of those who suffer but of oneself and those who are bystanders. Creative suffering leads to a victory that is part of the victory over the cosmic evil and part of the victory over the failures and oppressions of individuals.

In his letter to the church at Rome, the apostle Paul expresses this insight in a most profound way. What he states sets apart the contribution of the Judeo-Christian approach to suffering from that of the Eastern religions. Paul says, "I consider that the sufferings of this present time are not worth comparing with the glory that is to be revealed to us. For the creation . . . will be set free from its bondage to decay and obtain the glorious liberty of the children of God" (Rom. 8:19, 21).

In the Eastern religions, the goal is to be set free from the wheel of Karma to enter a Nirvana of nonexistence. To exist is to suffer, say the Eastern religions. For Paul, by contrast, the goal is to be set free from bondage to that which decays, and suffering (enduring) is the route. The freedom comes not from escape, but from a transformation of ourselves and our bodies.

For Paul, the secret lies in the fact that the Spirit of God has come into our midst—there is no need to try to reach the Spirit of God. This shared power of the Spirit allows us to know the ultimate result and gives us patience for the present. Even in our weakest moment, this Spirit teaches us how to pray. I take this to mean that when we are unable to find the way to symbolize so that we may succeed in our suffering work, there is a power that helps us find that way.

Paul therefore could say, and we can echo, even in the midst of suffering, "We know that everything works for good with those who love God, who are called according to God's purpose."

To that end, all of us who would help with the suffering moment must work. When we do, we have true ministry in the moment of suffering.

EPILOGUE

Toward a Theology of Responsibility

Suffering, whether personal or corporate, has a role in the victory over pain and evil. Those who care have a role. As the question of pain and the study of evil come to the fore, several implications grow out of this book.

The fundamental implication is found in the opening pages—the need to bring together the theology of liberation and that of the pastorate. Skills used in caring for the individual and skills used for intervening in the problems of society are different; yet they have much in common. We need now a genuine pastoral theology that pulls together the insights of practical theology and liberation theology. Until that integration is achieved, the full relevance of the Christian faith to life today will be missed.

The second implication grows from the first. As that integration takes place, this enlarged pastoral theology can and must speak to the other theological disciplines. *Encountering Evil*, edited by Stephen T. Davis, deals with various views of the theology of creation, the meaning of having in life both an all-powerful God and evil.[1] Yet, fine as that book is, it lacks the communication with pastoral theology that should inform it and also speak to the practice of ministry.

Such a contribution leads to what I would see as a theology of responsibility—the responsibility of the care giver, the responsibility of those who need healing, the responsibility of society, and, indeed, the responsibility of God!

Therefore, the call for a theology of responsibility is one purpose of this book. Sometimes the responsibility is to "shake the dust from your feet and move on," as Jesus once told his disciples. Sometimes the responsibility is to sacrifice oneself. Polycarp and many of the early church used that approach. Sometimes the responsibility is to overthrow—a responsibility of revolution. This was seen with Jesus in cleansing the temple and has come much alive in the last three centuries. And sometimes the responsibility is to be overthrown! Democracy is based on the view that a government in power must accept the responsibility to be overthrown when the electorate so dictates.

We need the art and the grace to know where and in what context these responses to the victory of Christ are appropriate. Pastoral theology, in both its psychological and sociological expressions, is the theology of that art. The art form discerns when the battle is cosmic, when local, when both. The art form knows when the battle requires confrontation and when the strategy demands facilitation.

True knowledge of this art comes only through God. We must develop that spirituality which allows for the victory over evil and then allows for responsible dealing with that victory.

Out of the dynamic of suffering comes, therefore, a call—a call not only to deal with suffering but a call for a theology of responsibility. It is my hope not only that this book may make some contribution to "suffering—its meaning and ministry," but that from that contribution, we may move on to a broader issue: a theology of responsibility informed by the suffering work of life. Amen.

NOTES

Introduction

1. In reviewing this book, I find that nowhere do I quote Victor Frankl directly. Yet the importance of the role of meaning in dealing with suffering must be identified as his great legacy to the field of counseling and care. For a general understanding of the place of meaning in the battle for survival, I commend the works of Dr. Frankl—especially his *Death Camp to Existentialism*.
2. Don Browning, *The Moral Context of Pastoral Care* (Philadelphia: Westminster Press, 1976).

I. Suffering: Nature, Meaning, Necessity

1. Seward Hiltner, *Preface to Pastoral Theology* (Nashville: Abingdon Press, 1958).
2. Paul Tillich, *The Courage to Be* (New Haven: Yale University Press, 1952).
3. James Emerson, *The Dynamics of Forgiveness* (Philadelphia: Westminster Press, 1964).

II. Biblical and Theological Views

1. Carl R. Rogers and Rosalind F. Dymond, *Psychotherapy and Personality Change* (University of Chicago Press, 1954).
2. Edward Schillebeeckx, *Jesus: An Experiment in Christology*, trans. Hoskins (New York: Seabury Press, 1979), pp. 44 ff.
3. Emerson, *Dynamics of Forgiveness*.

III. Psychological Dimensions

1. For background on the work of Abraham H. Maslow, the following book includes both selected works and a complete

bibliography: *The Farther Reaches of Human Nature* (New York: Viking Press, 1971). Maslow's basic concept of needs appeared in lectures and articles, and in his *Motivation and Personality* (New York: Harper & Row, 1954).

2. Erik Erickson, *Childhood and Society* (New York: W. W. Norton, 1964).
3. Kurt Lewin, *Field Theory in Social Science,* ed. Dorwin Cartwright (New York: Harper & Row, 1951).
4. On first reading, I understood Dorothee Söelle to hold that suffering means the absence of meaning. On further review, I believe that to be an incorrect reading of her view. I do believe, however, that her relegating of Calvin and the prayer of the Mass ("I am not worthy to come under the roof of your house") to a form of masochism misses the mark. Both can be used in masochistic ways, but both also can be avenues to meaning which affirms reality at a given point in the phases of suffering. Apart from that, her book stands as the finest statement on the subject of suffering I have seen. I do not repeat her material here, but commend the book as a theological discussion of what here is a "pastoral theological" discussion: *Suffering* (Philadelphia: Fortress Press, 1975), p. 23.
5. Harold S. Kushner, *When Bad Things Happen to Good People* (New York: Schocken Books, 1981), p. 18. In a book I appreciate both for its emergence from his own suffering and its help to my parishioners, I yet feel Kushner has not understood the role of mysticism. He quotes the prayer, "Tell me not why I must suffer. Assure me only that I suffer for Thy sake," and finds it "wanting." On the contrary, the assurance that there may be a solidarity in "my suffering" and "God's suffering" provides the ability to experience suffering work. Note Sölle's chapter on this point: *Suffering,* pp. 93 ff.
6. Archibald MacLeish, *J. B.* (Boston: Houghton Mifflin Co., 1956).
7. I first heard this concept from Dr. Kenneth Mitchell in 1980. Dr. Mitchell has served on the staffs of the Menninger Foundation, Topeka, Kansas; Dubuque Theological Seminary, Iowa; and Eden Theological Seminary, St. Louis, Missouri. I have not seen the concept developed in writing, but give him full credit for the metaphor, which I have found most helpful.
8. The polliwog example illustrates developmental stages; but I find some confusion as to whether the credit goes to Kurt Goldstein or to George Coghill. The background studies for understanding development are found in Goldstein's *The Organisms* (New York: American Book Co., 1939) and in Coghill's *Anatomy and the Problem of Behavior* (New York: Harper & Row, 1969).

9. This work took place in connection with a major study by The Community Service Society of New York City in 1970. The information comes from notes kept during my tenure as general director of that organization.
10. Elie Wiesel, *Night,* trans. Stella Rodway (New York: Hill & Wang, 1960), pp. 77 ff.

IV. Contemporary Views

1. Sölle, *Suffering,* pp. 70-74.
2. In the United States, William H. Willimon has written extensively in the field. In Germany, Hans-Joachim Thilo has given us a perceptive book, *Die therapeutische Funktion des Gottesdienstes* (Johannes Stauda Verlag, 1985).
3. In the development of this section, I am indebted to the comments and unpublished papers of John Beckham, William Bolger, Donna Deffke, and John Paul Jones of San Francisco, and John Sutherland Bonnell of New York. Except for the case study about "Bill," all the individual studies are composites from my own case studies and conversations with these people.

V. Suffering Healer—Healed Healer

1. For this observation of the true nature of *paradox,* credit goes to Professor Sergi Singh of San Francisco Theological Seminary, San Anselmo, California.
2. Any of the basic material of C. G. Jung deals with the shadow. A short and excellent introduction to the concept will be found in Jolande Jacobi, *The Psychology of C. G. Jung* (New Haven: Yale University Press, 1973), pp. 109-13.
3. William Somerset Maugham, "Rain," in *The Favorite Short Stories of William Somerset Maugham* (Garden City, N.Y.: Doubleday, 1937).
4. This shadow experience in the group is presented in composite form to provide anonymity.
5. Henri Nouwen, *The Wounded Healer* (Garden City, N.Y.: Doubleday, 1965).
6. The "seven last words" do not appear at any one place, but are gathered from the four Gospel accounts; most are found in Luke and John.
7. Martin Buber, *I and Thou,* trans. Ronald Smith (Edinburgh: T. & T. Clark; New York: Charles Scribner's Sons, 1937).
8. M. Scott Peck, *People of the Lie* (New York: Simon & Schuster, 1983), p. 174.
9. Emerson, *Dynamics of Forgiveness.*

VI. Symbols, Scripture, Strategy

1. Susan Langer, *Philosophy in a New Key* (Cambridge, Mass.: Harvard University Press, A Mentor Book, 1942).

Epilogue

1. Stephen T. Davis, ed., *Encountering Evil* (Atlanta: John Knox Press, 1981).

SUBJECT INDEX

SCRIPTURE INDEX